Shakespair

BOOKS OF ORIGINAL AND TRANSLATED VERSE
BY MARTIN BIDNEY

Series: East-West Bridge Builders

Volume I: *East-West Poetry:*
A Western Poet Responds to Islamic Tradition in Sonnets, Hymns, and Songs
State University of New York Press

Volume II: J. W. von Goethe, *East-West Divan:*
The Poems, with "Notes and Essays": Goethe's Intercultural Dialogues
(translation from the German with original verse commentaries)
State University of New York Press

Volume III: *Poems of Wine and Tavern Romance:*
A Dialogue with the Persian Poet Hafiz
(translated from von Hammer's German versions, with original verse commentaries)
State University of New York Press

Volume IV: *A Unifying Light:*
Lyrical Responses to the Qur'an
Dialogic Poetry Press

Other Books

Alexander Pushkin, *Like a Fine Rug of Erivan: West-East Poems*
(trilingual with audio, co-translated from Russian and
co-edited with Bidney's Introduction)
Mommsen Foundation / Global Scholarly Publications

Saul Tchernikhovsky, *Lyrical Tales and Poems of Jewish Life*
(translated from the Russian versions of Vladislav Khodasevich)
Keshet Press

A Poetic Dialogue with Adam Mickiewicz: The "Crimean Sonnets"
(translated from the Polish, with Sonnet Preface, Sonnet Replies, and Notes)
Bernstein-Verlag Bonn

Enrico Corsi and Francesca Gambino, *Divine Adventure: The Fantastic Travels of Dante*
(English verse rendition of the prose translation by Maria Vera Properzi-Altschuler)
Idea Publications

[For e-books of verse and works of criticism see martinbidney.com]

𝕾𝖍𝖆𝖐𝖊𝖘𝖕𝖆𝖎𝖗

Sonnet Replies to the 154 *Sonnets* of William Shakespeare

MARTIN BIDNEY

Dialogic
Poetry
Press

Copyright © 2015 by Martin Bidney
Vestal, New York

All Rights Reserved

ISBN 13: 978-1517697945
ISBN 10: 1517697948

Printed in the United States of America

DEDICATION

I gratefully will dedicate this book
To friends who have encouraged me the most
By reading sample sonnets that I wrote
And then, in helpful e-mail colloquies
With comments, offered kindly, in reply,
Interpretation and community
And friendship and refreshment and delight:

> Shahid Alam
> Jaimee Wriston Colbert
> Louise Fairfax
> Geoffrey Gould
> Anni Johnson
> Johanna Masters
> Katharina Mommsen
> Zoja Pavlovskis
> Philipp Restetzki
> Charlene Thomson
> Hanna Zacks

Contents

Introduction	ix
Key to Pronunciation	xvii
Tribute Sonnet	xviii
Sonnets and Replies	2
Final Thoughts: On Proofing *Shakespair*	311
Index of Personal Names in the Replies	313

Introduction

The *Sonnets* of William Shakespeare (published in 1609 but mostly written in the 1590s) offer surprises everywhere, but two big ones in particular. These relate to the plot and to the range of the poet's passionate feeling. The story line has the makings of a high suspense love drama, but the author wants, more crucially, to explore his thoughts on a myriad of topics in what feels like verse journaling—moody, mercurial, unpredictable, and intense. That's why the genre of the narrative hovers between a play and what we'd now call a psychological novel.

    Complicating both the dramatic tension and the introspective depth is the bisexual range of the poet's passionate temperament. The fact that his boyfriend and mistress are attracted to each other will account for some of the strong conflicts in the speaker's mind. But the wild oscillations of his feeling toward each of them are also rooted in his widely receptive sexual nature.

    Poetry, as imaginative art, is a species of fiction, so the speaker of the poetry is from this point of view a fictive persona. But William Shakespeare likes to make multiple wordplays on the name "Will," just as Marcel Proust, in his autobiographic novel, calls the protagonist "Marcel." Walter Cohen, in *The Norton Shakespeare* (based on the *Oxford*), finds the Will-persona so very Shakespeare-like that he even, quite understandably, calls the protagonist's affair with the ladyfriend "adulterous" because the poet was married. But the lady doesn't even enter the book till sonnet 40. Rather, Shakespeare begins sonnet 1 by likening his handsome boyfriend to "beauty's rose" and spends the first 39 poems urging his friend to have children, so the attractive legacy may be, as we now say, "paid forward." The boyfriend is likened to a rose several more times in later lyrics (sonnets 35, 54, 95, 98, 99, and especially 109); indeed the poet seems to have a rival who also writes up the same beloved man in poetry (sonnets 79–80, 83, 86). Though Hallett Smith, in *The Riverside Shakespeare*, points to sonnet 20 as proving the speaker has only strictly non-sexual, "platonic" love for the boyfriend, Smith doesn't choose to mention that the friend, called "master-mistress" of the poet's "passion," has a "woman's face," a "woman's heart," and was "first created" as "a woman." This theme ties in well the the rose metaphor since the appearance, texture, and structure of a rose have been felt, throughout the centuries, to be intensely evocative of female sexuality. It's helpful to recall that the person compared "to a summer's day," with its "darling" Maytime "buds," is also the boyfriend. In sonnet 53 he's both Adonis and Helen of Troy for perfect beauty: gender boundaries are fluid.

Indeed, for over a century it has become widely accepted in psychology that human sexuality is not governed by a law of clear, unquestionable demarcations, written on two tablets to command two mutually exclusive gender attractions. Rather, human sexuality is a continuum, a spectrum.

As regards plot, or what there is of it, the poet spends far more time writing love poetry to the man, even after the alluring woman has entered the picture. True, many poems, whether dealing with boyfriend or mistress, might perhaps better be called love-hate lyrics. In fact, Cohen further observes that in most of the sonnets the gender of the love object is never made explicit, so we tend to interpret it in terms of where we seem to be in the "plot." Cohen is also right, however, in stressing that, on balance, the speaker's attitudes toward the boyfriend are much more positive than the remarks addressed to, or depicting, the mistress.

In sum, *gender and genre attractions are in flux*. And so are the poet's ideas on the other topics treated—subjects that all, in their several ways, relate to the ups and downs of love: nature, seasons, time, death, poetry, survival, religion, humility, self-renouncing, and self-affirming. It gave me deep joy to have occasion to converse with "Will" on all of these in a dialogic verse-book.

I'm a dialogic poet, carrying on a long tradition of friendly rivalry among verse writers. The ancient Greek Olympics included musical competitions; and performing music, in the broad Hellenic sense, was thought no different from reciting lyric poems—writings you might chant to the lyre. The theory of the agon or contest that can spur artistic innovation has been reviving in the work of Harold Bloom, and I like to read his books for reliable invigoration—as Charles Ives read Emerson, or as Yeats read Nietzsche. When putting together a collection of dialogic verse-exchanges with a master poet, I imagine feeling as Picasso had felt in painting his variations on Goya's *Las Meninas*. Or—a more accurate and modest parallel—I'm an art student at the Louvre, devotedly copying an Old Master while gradually discovering something about my own developing abilities while doing it. What could better rouse the drive to heighten verse technique and to expand a horizon of imagining than the prospect of a dialogue with Shakespeare?

I found that anything I'd learned, in my more than seventy years of living (and thirty-five years of teaching literature), about psychology, philosophy, or poetic history might be called for at any moment as I tried to be a helpful conversation partner. Shakespeare—voracious reader, visionary pioneer, practical man of the world, incomparable student of human nature—is the most rewarding of all possible partners in dialogue. Also, as a violinist, choir member, and folk performer, I naturally noted another expression of the Bard's pre-eminence in lyric writing. A musician in words, he lived in England's golden age of songwriting, when a lyricist at court was likely, as well, to be a composer, vocalist, and lutanist or keyboard player: think of Thomas Campion, Orlando Gibbons, or—my favorite—John Dowland. In my twenties I spent hours listening to a Nonesuch LP of Dowland (it rhymes with Roland, which was often spelled "Rowland" in those days). His Latin motto, "Semper Dowland, semper dolens" ("Always Dowland, always grieving"), points to the lugubrious mood of his elegant madrigals, their grief made sweet. I bought Noah Greenberg's anthology of Elizabethan songs, too, and still love to sing the first Dowland lyric I memorized: "Flow, My Tears."

So I was prepared to appreciate the mellifluent craft of Shakespeare as a sonnet maker. But the thoroughgoing scope of that artisanry took me by surprise. Making vowel and consonant critiques of individual sonnets, I discovered that if any sound appeared once in a poem it was nearly certain to occur at least one other time. What might have been an anomaly when found alone becomes a harmony when encountered twice. The sonnets are all tightly harmonized on this hidden principle, and in my replies I've attempted a similar rigor—a strictness that is pure pleasure to maintain because the more attentively we care for Shakespeare's vocal art, the more alertly we will take in the spirit of his verbal singing.

Let me offer a bit of context in the matter of poetic dialogue as I've come to regard it. What you're holding is the latest in a series of books each containing poems-with-replies. I began with Polish lyrics in *A Poetic Dialogue with Adam Mickiewicz: The "Crimean Sonnets" Translated, with Sonnet Preface, Sonnet Replies, and Notes* (2007), and followed it with *East-West Poetry: A Western Poet Responds* to Islamic Tradition in Sonnets, Hymns, and Songs (2010), where I start most poems with an epigraph from the Qur'an. In a third dialogue project, *West-East Divan—The Poems, with "Notes and Essays": Goethe's Intercultural Dialogues* (2010), after translating 250 poems by Germany's finest poet, I responded with about 280 verse replies. Bold as the project was, reviewers in America and Germany have liked it, and selections were read last July in two programs on the BBC.

I hope the reader will agree it isn't much crazier to converse with Shakespeare than to have traded lyrics with Goethe. In some commentary poems I call the German poet simply "Brother Wolf," my fellow cultivator of the strophes, rhythms, and assonantal-alliterative patternings we both love well.

The point—an overwhelmingly important one, I think—is to show that traditional verse forms are not a dead language. They're not heard much anymore, but—why not? I'll be wanting to use them the rest of my life. There's no reason they should have to die. Any form ever used is available for writers to employ today—this minute. You can have the most intimate colloquies with people whose favorite literary techniques you love so much you want to use them many, many times. Every dialogue venture gives you a new persona when you write in the favored lyric forms of your colleague, friend, and mentor. You'll find that when you assumed a stranger-self it changed you, and it made a stranger you.

Another recent colloquy project of mine was *Poems of Wine and Tavern Romance: A Dialogue with the Persian Poet Hafiz* (2013). Here I converse with 103 lyrics of Hafiz as rendered into German by Joseph von Hammer (1814) and then into English by me. Hammer was a translator and poetic metrist of genius, and it was his version of Hafiz' *Divan*, the first ever made into any European language, that had inspired Goethe to publish his own "west-east" reply five years later. Hafiz—a medieval Sufi poet-monk who's drunk on love and wine—was yet another of the selves I wanted to inhabit for awhile. You can see that the making of dialogues in verse has now become my way of life.

In fact, a remarkable kinship suddenly appears to me between Muhammad Shemseddin Hafiz and William Shakespeare—two superb lyrical spirits, two bisexual bards. It appears that the range of each man's passion was distrusted or disapproved by early readers. In rendering Hafiz I had to correct the work of German translator Joseph von Hammer, who had often changed the gender of the addressees in the Persian love poems. Because Joachim Wohlleben's philological faithfulness and accurate scholarship luckily allowed me to do this without knowing Persian, I was surprised at the overwhelming number of poems suddenly addressed to male companions, though instead of a Shakespearean rose Hafiz is likelier to compare the male object of his affection to a narcissus. As for Shakespeare, Hallett Smith tells us that an editor named John Benson in 1640 altered poetic addressees' gender so that "most" of the poems that are spoken to a man seem, in the Benson edition, addressed to a woman. For "nearly 150 years" this was the edition of the *Sonnets* that "the world knew," not corrected till 1780 by Edmond Malone. I enjoy being able to help dispel the clouds of misperception. It has been observed that "the truth shall make you free."

As Shakespeare would be the first to concur, it's valuable to range widely in your interests. In my versing dialogue projects, I keep looking for more countries, cultures, and historical eras. More scriptures, more dictions, more rhythms, more resources. More facts, more ficts. But no factions in our fictions. The best outlook, the ideal mentality, for a dialogic poet would combine Emerson's "Self-Reliance" with his vision of ever widening friendship in "Circles."

When I gave a talk abut "lyrical replies" for the Retirees' Club of Binghamton University, my friend and colleague Francis X. Newman asked, "Have you considered writing replies to Shakespeare's *Sonnets*?"

Here they are. I converse with Shakespeare freely in the form he loved. His book of poems is the verse novel of a multiply conflicted adventure of the heart. The lively speaker-persona is one of the deepest, most revealing character-creations of Shakespearean drama. I react to what he says about himself and his problematic, much-loved friends. I don't speculate, though, about the real-life identity of the speaker's boyfriend, mistress, or rival. I would rather respond to individual poems as filled with thoughts and feelings volunteered by an enjoyable companion in conversation.

Often I sum up a lyric from what appears a new perspective, or I'll comment with parallel or contrasting memories and imaginings of my own. Poets, philosophers, mythic figures, musicians, or novelists may enter my replies. Psychological sidelights will be many. The possibilities revealed by the genre of lyrical response appear unlimited. Making a dialogue book with Shakespeare taught me more about sonnet writing, about the ever-changing state of mind it opens up, than any other training could possibly have done—a challenge with alacrity accepted.

References

Cohen, Walter. "The Sonnets and 'A Lover's Complaint,'" pp. 1915–1922 in *The Norton Shakespeare Based on the Oxford Edition* (Norton, New York: 1997), Stephen Greenblatt, General Editor; see 1915, 1919.

Smith, Hallett. "Sonnets," pp. 1839–1842 in *The Riverside Shakespeare*, second edition (Boston: Houghton Mifflin, 1997), G. Blakemore Evans, General and Textual Editor; see 1840, 1841–42.

Key to Pronunciation

𝕴n this edition the words in the Shakespeare poems are spelled in a way that clarifies their pronunciation so the intended rhythm can be enjoyably heard. When a syllable is not intended to be pronounced, an apostrophe is substituted: "flattery" will become "flatt'ry"; "despised" will become "despis'd." However, the poet often wanted the syllable "-ed" to be pronounced at the ends of words. *So when you see the ending "ed" always pronounce it.* The word "buried" will have three syllables: "bu-ri-ed." The word "disabled" will have four syllables: "dis-a-bl-ed." This rule keeps the rhythm clear and strong. And it makes it possible to hear the end rhymes of lines, too. Sonnet 31 begins with a quatrain that I'll help you recite right now by using hyphens:

> Thy bosom is endear-ed with all hearts,
> Which I by lacking have suppos-ed dead;
> And there reigns Love, and all Love's loving parts,
> And all those friends which I thought buri-ed.

When Shakespeare wants a two-syllable "even" I'll write it as "even." When he wants only one syllable, I'll write "ev'n." Also, when nowadays we stress a word differently than Shakespeare did, I'll use a stress mark to show how he said it: "revenue" becomes "revénue."

Tribute Sonnet
to my friend William Shakespeare

From reading proofs I need a little break
And thus to my computer rush, to write
(That I may utter praise, not merely take
But give—to one occasioning delight)

Of my response in composition. Might
I quickly be permitted to awake
The grateful sense within of dawning light
That blazing strong the sun-blond locks will shake!

Of heart-blood and the flood of henna hue
My *cármina* may carmine color hint
That complements the lofting up of dew
When, sunlike in the humbler eye, the glint

    Of insight, pearl of liquid light in you,
    Means quill of bird on screen of print I view.

Shakespair

Sonnet 1

From fairest creatures we desire increase,
That thereby beauty's rose might never die,
But as the riper should by time decease,
His tender heir might bear his memory.

But thou, contracted to thine own bright eyes,
Feed'st thy light's flame with self-substantial fuel,
Making a famine where abundance lies,
Thyself thy foe, to thy sweet self too cruel.

Thou that art now the world's fresh ornament
And only herald to the gaudy spring,
Within thine own bud buriest thy content,
And, tender churl, mak'st waste in niggarding:

    Pity the world, or else this glutton be,
    To eat the world's due, by the grave and thee.

Reply

The beauty-rose? A man. Remarkable.
Another man is telling him that he
Had best beget, lest love might die with full
Ascent unrealized, a penury,

Though cloaked in seeming riches: "If, self-prized,
You nothing sowed, lived unproductively,
Regardless of the offspring dreamed, despised
As barren death's own narrow home you'd be."

Who doesn't wish to give, but shyly keeps
(The miser!) what is in him to bestow
In unawakened enervation sleeps
That will not let the "I" or others grow.

    For love must lend. Remain neglectful of
    The giving-wisdom, and you'll never love.

Sonnet 2

When forty winters shall besiege thy brow
And dig deep trenches in thy beauty's field,
Thy youth's proud livery, so gaz'd on now,
Will be a tatter'd weed of small worth held.

Then being ask'd where all thy beauty lies,
Where all the treasure of thy lusty days,
To say within thine own deep sunken eyes
Were an all-eating shame and thriftless praise.

How much more praise deserv'd thy beauty's use
If thou couldst answer, 'This fair child of mine
Shall sum my count, and make my old excuse,'
Proving his beauty by succession thine!

    This were to be new made when thou art old
    And see thy blood warm when thou feel'st it cold.

Reply

Though here the lesson barely differs from
The earlier we heard—first metaphor
From rose new-altered, having now become
A money-hunger emblem—how much more

Warm-wonderful the final lines' relief
(The bland cash calculations being done),
Recalling sap in spring, and branching leaf,
Well heated by the propagating sun.

The parable of talents left me cold.
Investment? Let it feel more genitive:
More handsome, gladder spending than the gold
Is laying out what heart's blood fain would give,

    New-manned by view of upright cedar tree
    That rising youth will let you heightened see.

Sonnet 3

Look in thy glass and tell the face thou viewest
Now is the time that face should form another,
Whose fresh repair if now thou not renewest,
Thou dost beguile the world, unbless some mother.

For where is she so fair whose unear'd womb
Disdains the tillage of thy husbandry?
Or who is he so fond will be the tomb
Of his self-love to stop posterity?

Thou art thy mother's glass, and she in thee
Calls back the lovely April of her prime;
So thou through windows of thine age shalt see,
Despite of wrinkles, this thy golden time.

> But if thou live remember'd not to be,
> Die single and thine image dies with thee.

Reply

One might have thought that we were listening
To mere entreaty-writing to Narcissus.
The forfeiture of image is a thing
To fear: a fond posterity will miss us

That might have loved our mirror-picture. So
Ignored, nymph Echo fitly pleaded with
The me-admirer who dismissed her woe,
Cries' cold reverberation into myth

Belied by wailing for his icy eyes.
The lake where he had stared is like a glass
Where dumbly summons in a brighter guise
A chill rigidity, a sand morass,

> Mimetic rhetoric a chidden charm—
> Betrayal glacial—guarded, hidden harm.

Sonnet 4

Unthrifty loveliness, why dost thou spend
Upon thy self thy beauty's legacy?
Nature's bequest gives nothing, but doth lend,
And being frank she lends to those are free:

Then, beauteous niggard, why dost thou abuse
The bounteous lárgess given thee to give?
Profitless usurer, why dost thou use
So great a sum of sums, yet canst not live?

For having traffic with thy self alone,
Thou of thyself thy sweet self dost deceive:
Then how when nature calls thee to be gone,
What ácceptable audit canst thou leave?

    Thy unus'd beauty must be tomb'd with thee,
    Which, used, lives th' executor to be.

Reply

Executor and executioner—
Bequest or death: one cannot help but choose.
You've heard that rule before, but we prefer
To rail, relentless, let you not refuse!

Your venture capital will get no wage
If not invested—capital offense.
So mortgage assets that, by mortal gauge,
Earned profit early may reward good sense.

A self-regarding passion merely means
The bills that bear your image cannot pay.
Who proudly in the dreaming-mirror preens
Will find his mintage melted quite away.

> Be shamed who thus can liquidate accounts:
> As income dwindles, debt unpaid yet mounts.

Sonnet 5

Those hours that with gentle work did frame
The lovely gaze where every eye doth dwell
Will play the tyrants to the very same,
And that unfair which fairly doth excel;

For never-resting time leads summer on
To hideous winter and confounds him there,
Sap check'd with frost and lusty leaves quite gone,
Beauty o'er-snow'd and bareness everywhere.

Then were not summer's distillation left,
A liquid pris'ner pent in walls of glass,
Beauty's effect with beauty were bereft,
Nor it, nor no remembrance what it was:

> But flow'rs distill'd, though they with winter meet,
> Leese but their show; their substance still lives sweet.

Reply

Perpetuate the summer in perfume.
The play of aromatic atmosphere
When loosed within the chilly living room
Revives, for old times' sake, the waning year.

Elusive as the trailing flame that links
The rubies, faceted, on table spread,
Yet more intense the fragrance that one drinks
From crystal phial of the flower-bed.

Insemination-lesson put aside
That still the poet chiefly would enforce,
Another kind of child may here abide:
Let mental propagation take its course.

    Attention concentrate! You'll then produce
    What your essential lyric will unloose.

Sonnet 6

Then let not winter's ragged hand deface
In thee thy summer ere thou be distill'd:
Make sweet some vial; treasure thou some place
With beauty's treasure ere it be self-kill'd.

That use is not forbidden usury
Which happies those that pay the willing loan;
That's for thyself to breed another thee,
Or ten times happier, be it ten for one.

Ten times thyself were happier than thou art,
If ten of thine ten times refigur'd thee:
Then what could death do if thou shouldst depart,
Leaving thee living in posterity?

    Be not self-will'd, for thou art much too fair
    To be death's conquest and make worms thine
       heir.

Reply

Ten children—quite an order. How shall *we*
Regard this unrelenting sermon-urge?
It's not too foreign to the likes of me
Who with a singer's lyring-drive would merge.

I want to copy writers whom I love
And pleased would be their minds to multiply:
Let in my lines appear the image of
The one who shines, abiding, in the sky.

Ten children? Books, when one this meaning picks...
That would indeed be fine—or many more,
Each mirroring in doubled picture-mix
The one who writes and him that wrote before.

    Spry scions, imaged multiplicities,
    Abundant suns of wonder, young one sees.

Sonnet 7

𝔏o! in the orient when the gracious light
Lifts up his burning head, each under eye
Doth homage to his new-appearing sight,
Serving with looks his sacred majesty;

And having climb'd the steep-up heav'nly hill,
Resembling strong youth in his middle age,
Yet mortal looks adore his beauty still,
Attending on his golden pilgrimage.

But when from highmost pitch, with weary car,
Like feeble age, he reeleth from the day,
The eyes, 'fore duteous, now converted are
From his low tract, and look another way:

    So thou, thyself outgoing in thy noon,
    Unlook'd on, di'st unless thou get a son.

Reply

The sun, for David, as the groom appears
That from his wedding chamber comes refreshed,
Or like a strong man running, to the cheers,
Perhaps, of clapping throng. The two are meshed

When here a man is told to have a son
To compensate for weakening in age.
And yet the dying sky's not always dun
Or dull, but high titanic war might wage:

Emboldened hydral night in bloody roar
May strive with light in final agony.
In chaos, even—stained in battle-gore—
The lordly oriflammes of cavalry

    A glory symbolize of older time
    Before the leaves were covered, cold, in rime.

Sonnet 8

Music to hear, why hear'st thou music sadly?
Sweets with sweets war not, joy delights in joy:
Why lov'st thou that which thou receiv'st not gladly
Or else receiv'st with pleasure thine annoy?

If the true concord of well-tuned sounds,
By unions marri'd, do offend thine ear,
They do but sweetly chide thee, who confounds
In singleness the parts that thou shouldst bear.

Mark how one string, sweet husband to another,
Strikes each in each by mutual ordering,
Resembling sire and child and happy mother
Who, all in one, one pleasing note do sing—

    Whose speechless song being many, seeming one,
    Sings this to thee: 'Thou single wilt prove none.'

Reply

Let music lovers heartened be that I'm
The harp of conjugal felicity.
Unintermittently in all my rhyme
The theme's familial polyphony,

Whose tuning's empathetical vibration
Where discords, coming but to be resolved,
Resounding in reciprocal laudation,
Absolve from solitude each one involved.

Pythagoras proclaimed that all is number—
One, two, three, four—that add to final ten,
Perfection-total broached already. When
Will you, in major scale, awake from slumber?

    Become the leading tone to reach the key—
    Strong modal chord, awarded progeny.

Sonnet 9

Is it for fear to wet a widow's eye
That thou consum'st thyself in single life?
Ah! if thou issueless shalt hap to die,
The world will wail thee like a makeless wife;

The world will be thy widow and still weep
That thou no form of thee hast left behind
When every private widow well may keep,
By children's eyes, her husband's shape in mind.

Look! what an unthrift in the world doth spend
Shifts but his place, for still the world enjoys it;
But beauty's waste hath in the world an end
And, kept unus'd, the user so destroys it.

> No love toward others in that bosom sits
> That on himself such murd'rous shame commits.

Reply

Offense against the "world" a "sin" may be…
The progeny-concern—how biblical!
(God intervened, saved Sarah. Later He
Did that for Hannah. Barren womb, be full.)

But why direct the agitated ire
Against one victim out of all the rest?
Perhaps an anguished, banked-up passion fire
Is bright for one the writer loved the best.

Mere singleness a crime? I can't grasp why
Unless the love of woman would allow
The poet's comrade to identify
With him more fully than he can right now:

> Reflected in the graceful lady-eyes,
> The lover loves, the friend identifies.

Sonnet 10

For shame deny that thou bear'st love to any,
Who for thy self art so unprovident.
Grant, if thou wilt, thou art belov'd of many,
But that thou none lov'st is most evident:

For thou art so possess'd with murd'rous hate
That 'gainst thy self thou stick'st not to conspire,
Seeking that beauteous roof to ruinate
Which to repair should be thy chief desire.

O change thy thought, that I may change my mind:
Shall hate be fairer lodg'd than gentle love?
Be, as thy presence is, gracious and kind,
Or to thyself at least kind-hearted prove.

    Make thee another self for love of me,
    That beauty still may live in thine or thee.

Reply

Can't love yourself? You'll then be loving none,
For others love you, and the thing they love
You patently despise, yet are the one
Whose beauty means that you're most worthy of

The feeling that you lack. What proved self-hate?
The fact you need no children, want them not.
I dream to see their beauty! It is great,
Ev'n in my crazed and phantasmatic thought.

For everything you make must be adored
Who are amazingly unloving to
The worshiper bowed down before his lord:
He smitten will remain in loving you.

    When more endeared, you're more indifferent
    To him unrisen, grim, in prison pent.

Sonnet 11

As fast as thou shalt wane, so fast thou grow'st,
In one of thine, from that which thou departest;
And that fresh blood which youngly thou bestow'st
Thou mayst call thine when thou from youth
    convertest.

Herein lives wisdom, beauty, and increase;
Without this, folly, age, and cold decay:
If all were minded so, the times should cease,
And threescore year would make the world away.

Let those whom nature hath not made for store,
Harsh, featureless, and rude, barrenly perish:
Look, whom she best endow'd, she gave thee more—
Which bounteous gift thou shouldst in bounty
    cherish.

    She carv'd thee for her seal, and meant thereby
    Thou shouldst print more, not let that copy die.

Reply

The adoration of a beauty by
The speaker more and more has made it clear
The latter cannot but identify
With husband-prospect, in a coupling dear

As the imagined progeny. The seal
Is not an imprint only but a melt
Of wax to add to what the loved may feel
A testament of what the lover felt.

A seal upon the heart, upon the arm,
The suitor was in Solomonic song.
For love, more strong than death, undoes that harm,
If only giving let the love be long.

    Your signet polyphilic signifies
    By one blest image resting in the eyes.

Sonnet 12

When I do count the clock that tells the time
And see the brave day sunk in hideous night,
When I behold the violet past prime
And sable curls all silvered o'er with white,

When lofty trees I see barren of leaves
Which erst from heat did canopy the herd,
And summer's green all girded up in sheaves
Borne on the bier with white and bristly beard,

Then of thy beauty do I question make
That thou among the wastes of time must go,
Since sweets and beauties do themselves forsake
And die as fast as they see others grow;

> And nothing 'gainst Time's scythe can make defence
> Save breed, to brave him when he takes thee hence.

Reply

If soon we tire of unrelenting plaints
("Ah, heedless, lacking children!") best not chide
The speaker nonetheless. Life, when it faints,
Requires that offspring of some kind abide.

The record of fine works to leave behind,
Or emanations brave in grateful verse,
As well as issue physical may bind
Some future youth our mem'ries to rehearse.

Our children or appreciators we
Will need, who dithyrambic hymn can sound:
May, in a reconciling legacy,
We then arise from exile in the ground!

>   Delay the scythe, if it arrive to reap—
>   Let seed succeed, awaked from seeming sleep.

Sonnet 13

O that you were yourself! But, love, you are
No longer yours than you yourself here live:
Against this coming end you should prepare
And your sweet semblance to some other give.

So should that beauty which you hold in lease
Find no determination; then you were
Yourself again after yourself's decease,
When your sweet issue your sweet form should bear.

Who lets so fair a house fall to decay,
Which husbandry in honour might uphold
Against the stormy gusts of winter's day
And barren rage of death's eternal cold?

    O none but unthrifts! Dear my love, you know,
    You had a father: let your son say so.

Reply

The metaphor is ever altering.
The one belov'd is here the renter whose
Collapsing home will be foreclosed, a thing
That will evoke the fear of what he'd lose.

A poet feeling age apace advance
The peril knows, and so may well be warned:
We have to chance the reign of happenstance,
But find it grateful to be later mourned—

And greater, to be loved beyond the grave.
By husbanding ripe store in thriving child
You daily will be gaining what you gave
In dividends to drive a miser wild—

>   But only if, a million miles above
>   All profit motive, grow the life of love.

Sonnet 14

Not from the stars do I my judgement pluck,
And yet methinks I have astronomy,
But not to tell of good or evil luck,
Of plagues, of dearths, or seasons' quality,

Nor can I fortune to brief minutes tell,
'Pointing to each his thunder, rain, and wind,
Or say with princes if it shall go well
By oft predict that I in heaven find.

But from thine eyes my knowledge I derive,
And, constant stars, in them I read such art
As truth and beauty shall together thrive
If from thyself to store thou wouldst convert,

> Or else of thee this I prognosticate:
> Thy end is truth's and beauty's doom and date.

Reply

Is beauty truth, truth beauty? Only when
Can constellation, countenance combine
Attractiveness and faithful forecast. Then
Both, coessentially enduring, shine.

The astrological prediction can
Participate in that Platonic being
If it can but foretell another man
In whom will dwell the comely sight we're seeing.

But truth and loveliness together die
If eye-star tidings be not beautiful.
For no survival will these Gemini
Enable save by double stellar pull.

    Deter disaster—basking basilisk—
    And dare to propagate. Gone, aster-risk!

Sonnet 15

When I consider every thing that grows
Holds in perfection but a little moment,
That this huge stage presenteth nought but shows
Whereon the stars in secret influence comment,

When I perceive that men as plants increase,
Cheered and check'd ev'n by the selfsame sky,
Vaunt in their youthful sap, at height decrease,
And wear their brave state out of memory,

Then the conceit of this inconstant stay
Sets you most rich in youth before my sight
Where wasteful Time debateth with decay
To change your day of youth to sulli'd night;

    And all in war with Time for love of you,
    As he takes from you, I engraft you new.

Reply

𝔍 here will be the bard as gardener
And graft and gladly mold the cultivar
Of matching words for growth we most prefer
To further. As our floricultures are

In bowered writing one, will be our debts
Irrevocable, ever intertwined.
So Homer's winter-minstrel line begets
A bard-Ulysses artfully designed

For springtime. Better yet, Penelope,
Who faithful waits for her returning lord,
Fit image-wealth affords, depicting me:
Verse-graft and stem-plant stand in full accord,

    With blended hardy strength in garden bed,
    Rhymed lines by one another comforted.

Sonnet 16

But wherefore do not you a mightier way
Make war upon this bloody tyrant, Time,
And fortify your self in your decay
With means more blessed than my barren rhyme?

Now stand you on the top of happy hours,
And many maiden gardens, yet unset,
With virtuous wish would bear your living flowers,
Much liker than your painted counterfeit:

So should the lines of life that life repair,
Which this, Time's pencil, or my pupil pen,
Neither in inward worth nor outward fair,
Can make you live yourself in eyes of men.

> To give away yourself keeps yourself still,
> And you must live drawn by your own sweet skill.

Reply

While delving, being led suspensefully,
Deciphering obsessive diaries,
I enter, blend, then travel back, to see
How might it feel to live in thoughts like these,

I have to ask if he, the highest bard,
Most fertile in poetic progeny,
May find it not indeed a trifle hard
To hint mere fallow field or barren tree.

Though it be right forever to prefer
The living over things that cannot breathe,
Yet breath-winds lend respiring voyager
On sonnet seas an eager will to wreathe

    In verdant circlet of unfading bay
    The one who mind made sail, bright senses play.

Sonnet 17

Who will believe my verse in time to come
If it were fill'd with your most high deserts?
Though yet heav'n knows it is but as a tomb
Which hides your life and shows not half your parts.

If I could write the beauty of your eyes
And in fresh numbers number all your graces,
The age to come would say, 'This poet lies;
Such heavenly touches ne'er touch'd earthly faces.'

So should my papers, yellow'd with their age,
Be scorn'd, like old men of less truth than tongue,
And your true rights be term'd a poet's rage
And stretched metre of an antique song:

> But were some child of yours alive that time,
> You should live twice: in it, and in my rhyme.

Reply

It didn't take our poet long to show
Awareness of the fair objection I
Had noted. Fertile couplets, he must know,
As children stand—two gems, or Gemini.

His lines he still called lies, or overwrought
Embroidered laudatory rhetoric,
Yet we divine the true admirer's thought:
Child-equaling's in vain, a writer's trick.

But rhymes outlive a scion. Future time
May read the fruitful words upon a page
And feel warm youth infuse the paradigm
With all the blind refused in fighting age

> By staying single-minded. Panegyric
> May not awake him, yet survive in lyric.

Sonnet 18

Shall I compare thee to a summer's day?
Thou art more lovely and more temperate;
Rough winds do shake the darling buds of May,
And summer's lease hath all too short a date.

Sometime too hot the eye of heaven shines,
And often is his gold complexion dimm'd,
And every fair from fair sometime declines,
By chance, or nature's changing course untrimm'd;

But thy eternal summer shall not fade
Nor lose possession of that fair thou ow'st,
Nor shall death brag thou wander'st in his shade
When in eternal lines to time thou grow'st.

    So long as men can breathe or eyes can see,
    So long lives this, and this gives life to thee.

Reply

More lovely than a summer and the bloom
Of darling buds that may by winds be marred,
The man is made more loved in lyric room
Wherein he lives in beauty yet unscarred.

The soaring lines are by the reader known
As well as lyric hymn of later date
Regarding true love lost when blossoms blown
Are shaken down, that's yet a finer fate

Than "never to have loved at all." So we
Who gladly chant the lines we like to cite
Might well recall—each lover-melody
Will laud two friends' perpetual delight:

    A sacred bliss and brave—dear benison
    Of men that Shakespeare shares with Tennyson.

Sonnet 19

Devouring Time, blunt thou the lion's paws,
And make the earth devour her own sweet brood;
Pluck the keen teeth from the fierce tiger's jaws,
And burn the long-liv'd phoenix in her blood.

Make glad and sorry seasons as thou fleets,
And do whate'er thou wilt, swift-footed Time,
To the wide world and all her fading sweets;
But I forbid thee one most heinous crime:

O carve not with thy hours my love's fair brow
Nor draw no lines there with thine antique pen;
Him in thy course untainted do allow
For beauty's pattern to succeeding men.

    Yet, do thy worst, old Time: despite thy wrong,
    My love shall in my verse ever live young.

Reply

So antic-ancient is the pen of Time
And of the Poet, who in rivalry
Confounding young and old, in frost and rhyme,
Compound their playfulness with majesty!

"Time writes no wrinkle on thine azure brow,"
Had Byron claimed, when speaking to the sea:
Cavorting sportive energies allow
For waves and winds of creativity.

The tidal flows of time are like the act
Of breathing, tension freed by relaxation—
A strain of music is a flowing-fact:
Inbreathing upbeat, downbeat exhalation.

> New-old, emboldened, sounds the pounding heart,
> The pleasure of our life and measured art.

Sonnet 20

A woman's face with nature's own hand painted
Hast thou, the master-mistress of my passion;
A woman's gentle heart, but not acquainted
With shifting change as is false women's fashion;

An eye more bright than theirs, less false in rolling,
Gilding the object whereupon it gazeth;
A man in hue, all hues in his controlling,
Which steals men's eyes and women's souls
    amazeth.

And for a woman wert thou first created,
Till Nature, as she wrought thee, fell a-doting,
And by addition me of thee defeated
By adding one thing to my purpose nothing.

> But since she prick'd thee out for women's
>   pleasure,
> Mine be thy love and thy love's use their
>   treasure.

Reply

One added organ has the androgyne
Unneeded for the spiritual love
The smitten poet cultivates. A fine
Summation is afforded: writing of

The double-gendered rare attractiveness
In the prodigious wizardry of one
Whom all admire will profit lyre no less
Than women's opportunity for fun.

The Mona Lisa, Bacchus, Anne, and John
Depict one riddling enigmatic smile—
Platonic Leonardo leads you on,
Dualities that daunt to reconcile.

> Here man was woman first, then changed in state.
> (Man erst; the Sistine Sybil-Lady late.)

Sonnet 21

So is it not with me as with that Muse
Stirr'd by a painted beauty to his verse,
Who heav'n itself for ornament doth use
And every fair with his fair doth rehearse,

Making a couplement of proud compare,
With sun and moon, with earth and sea's rich gems,
With April's first-born flow'rs, and all things rare
That heaven's air in this huge rondure hems.

O let me, true in love, but truly write,
And then believe me, my love is as fair
As any mother's child, though not so bright
As those gold candles fix'd in heaven's air.

> Let them say more that like of hearsay well;
> I will not praise that purpose not to sell.

Reply

Cosmetic promptings paired with cosmic props
Convey the bale of baneful arrogation:
Addition artificial overtops
With spurious plumage tasteful moderation.

Comparisons of universal range
May pose a problem independently
Of what in beauty's due to artful change.
If poet will promote the object he

Desires to height of heaven, we will find
The superlunar stature claimed may be
Too aether-like to suit our sod-born mind—
So Beatrice became Theology,

> Appearing bloodless in the upper blue
> Where even Dante's giv'n but *distant* view.

Sonnet 22

My glass shall not persuade me I am old
So long as youth and thou are of one date;
But when in thee time's furrows I behold,
Then look I death my days should expiate.

For all that beauty that doth cover thee
Is but the seemly raiment of my heart,
Which in thy breast doth live, as thine in me:
How can I then be elder than thou art?

O therefore, love, be of thyself so wary
As I, not for myself, but for thee will,
Bearing thy heart, which I will keep so chary
As tender nurse her babe from faring ill.

> Presume not on the heart when mine is slain:
> Thou gav'st me thine not to give back again.

Reply

If these two gentlemen have traded hearts,
Can we conclude they've traded bodies, too?
So it would seem, exchange of inner parts
Implied (one claimed) exchanging what's on view.

It's all a rather complicated way
To beg, "Be careful! I identify
With how you may appear: do not dismay
The one who mirrors you within his eye."

We note the wit called "metaphysical"
In British poets who are styled "baroque"
In Europe. Intellect exerts a pull
On passion linked in metaphoric yoke.

    In later decades, many found it fun:
    Traherne, Vaugh'n, Herbert—Crashaw, Cowley,
        Donne.

Sonnet 23

As an unperfect actor on the stage
Who with his fear is put beside his part,
Or some fierce thing replete with too much rage
Whose strength's abundance weakens his own heart,

So I, for fear of trust, forget to say
The perfect ceremony of love's rite
And in mine own love's strength seem to decay,
O'ercharg'd with burthen of mine own love's might.

O let my looks be then the eloquence
And dumb presagers of my speaking breast,
Who plead for love, and look for recompense
More than that tongue that more hath more
      express'd.

    O learn to read what silent love hath writ:
    To hear with eyes belongs to love's fine wit.

Reply

It might feel odd to think of Shakespeare shy
Or tongue-tied. But the speaking man is not
The bard. The former, diffident, may fly
Although the latter's wise in hardy thought.

Superiority of tonelessness
Remains an entertaining paradox
In one whom rhyming gifts divine would bless.
Can anyone be candid when he mocks

That fright? Yet Gorgon face on Roman tomb
Was thought to grant the soul postmortal pow'r:
Should one's own overgrown emotions loom
And barring out effective exit, lour,

> An inward-facing Gorgon, mortal fear,
> Will make the need for mental weapons clear.

Sonnet 24

Mine eye hath play'd the painter and hath stell'd
Thy beauty's form in table of my heart;
My body is the frame wherein 'tis held,
And pérspective it is best painter's art.

For through the painter must you see his skill
To find where your true image pictur'd lies,
Which in my bosom's shop is hanging still,
That hath his windows glazed with thine eyes.

Now see what good turns eyes for eyes have done:
Mine eyes have drawn thy shape, and thine for me
Are windows to my breast, wherethrough the sun
Delights to peep, to gaze therein on thee.

> Yet eyes this cunning want to grace their art:
> They draw but what they see, know not the heart.

Reply

The play of eyes and images and of
Reflections, eye in eye, and points of view
Is clever, but may hide what joying love
Would like to clarify: a longing to

Behold reflected back in kindly eyes
Belonging's light enlivening the smile.
You then may tell what strength in friendship vies,
Your image witnessing that you beguile

The fine companion. Grateful, ample fire!—
We know what's meant in lines by William Blake:
"The lineaments of gratified desire."
All trick-perspective gone, there's no mistake:

> The eye limns heart when mirroring the glad
> Effect each partner on the other had.

Sonnet 25

Let those who are in favour with their stars
Of public honour and proud titles boast,
Whilst I, whom fortune of such triumph bars,
Unlook'd for joy in that I honour most.

Great princes' favourites their fair leaves spread
But as the marigold at the sun's eye,
And in themselves their pride lies buried,
For at a frown they in their glory die.

The painful warrior famouséd for fight,
After a thousand victories once foil'd,
Is from the book of honour razed quite,
And all the rest forgot for which he toil'd:

>Then happy I, that love and am belov'd,
>Where I may not remove nor be remov'd.

Reply

Here fame and honor are affairs of state,
Unstable. On obligatory bows
To public or to reigning potentate
That fate depends whose favor gain allows.

Though private, rare esteem if meetly shared
Makes richer than a privy councilor
The one whose caring isn't daily aired.
Sincere the predilections they prefer

Whose faith is all in mutuality.
How horrid!—forcing of a smile for show;
How vain!—constrained and painted chivalry;
How sad!—the vassal eye's factitious glow:

> Be thankful, now, for proud equality,
> The tankard hoisting joyful, boist'rously!

Sonnet 26

Lord of my love, to whom in vassalage
Thy merit hath my duty strongly knit,
To thee I send this written embassage
To witness duty, not to show my wit:

Duty so great, which wit so poor as mine
May make seem bare in wanting words to show it,
But that I hope some good conceit of thine
In thy soul's thought, all naked, will bestow it,

Till whatsoever star that guides my moving
Points on me graciously with fair aspéct,
And puts apparel on my tatter'd loving
To show me worthy of thy sweet respect.

> Then may I dare to boast how I do love thee;
> Till then, not show my head where thou mayst
> prove me.

Reply

The commentator's lot? It isn't easy.
The crabbéd strife within the diaries,
Unsyllogistic, made logicians queasy,
And here we sample a supreme unease.

The prior sonnet fairly would proclaim
Pure freedom from a princely entourage
When caring, shared, is favored over fame—
Yet here equality's a sheer mirage.

A skittish, nervous insecurity
Has made the lyrist derogate the song
Where late he shone, to laud the panoply
Of stellar might as guide to right and wrong.

> The "negatively capable," though praised,
> May leave the brain dismayed or faintly dazed.

Sonnet 27

Weary with toil, I haste me to my bed,
The dear respose for limbs with travel tir'd;
But then begins a journey in my head
To work my mind when body's work's expir'd,

For then my thoughts—from far where I abide—
Intend a zealous pilgrimage to thee,
And keep my drooping eyelids open wide,
Looking on darkness which the blind do see:

Save that my soul's imaginary sight
Presents thy shadow to my sightless view,
Which, like a jewel hung in ghastly night,
Makes black night beauteous and her old face new.

    Lo! thus by day my limbs, by night my mind,
    For thee, and for myself, no quiet find.

Reply

"For she doth hang upon the cheek of night
Like a rich jewel in an Ethiop's ear,"
So that the mind of Romeo, bedight
With Juliet's adorning gleam, no fear

Need feel. Here, too, the thinker's pilgrim-tryst
Made glad the dark that frames remembered rays
Enriched so far that little will be missed
And prosper light in promised lyric praise.

Excitement heightening both night and sun,
The wanderer that walks on earth or air
When daytime laboring at length is done
Will celebrate in sky a friendship fair.

    It is a tiredness one may well admire
    That light re-livens with celestial fire.

Sonnet 28

How can I then return in happy plight,
That am debarr'd the benefit of rest
When day's oppression is not eas'd by night,
But day by night and night by day oppress'd,

And each, though enemies to either's reign,
Do in consent shake hands to torture me,
The one by toil, the other to complain
How far I toil, still farther off from thee?

I tell the day to please him thou art bright,
And dost him grace when clouds do blot the heaven;
So flatter I the swart-complexion'd night
When sparkling stars twire not thou gild'st the even.

> But day doth daily draw my sorrows longer,
> And night doth nightly make grief's strength seem stronger.

Reply

We here lament, in odd reverse again,
What we were gladly lauding latterly.
The final couplet might have hinted, then,
The shift that should surprise no longer be.

Two-liner endings with delight can serve
A double function: summing up the gist—
Or coming in, abrupt, with sudden swerve—
Or both at once, indeed (this may be missed!).

Petrarchan changes gradually turn
From first to second part, no lightning bolt.
Eight lines, then six, will leisure lend to learn
New genesis of mood, without a jolt.

> But, with eruptive lunge, a quick-wit quip
> In whirling hurtle-world the word will whip.

Sonnet 29

When, in disgrace with fortune and men's eyes,
I all alone beweep my outcast state,
And trouble deaf heav'n with my bootless cries,
And look upon myself and curse my fate,

Wishing me like to one more rich in hope,
Featur'd like him, like him with friends possess'd,
Desiring this man's art, and that man's scope,
With what I most enjoy contented least,

Yet in these thoughts myself almost despising,
Haply I think on thee, and then my state,
Like to the lark at break of day arising
From sullen earth, sings hymns at heaven's gate;

> For thy sweet love remember'd such wealth brings
> That then I scorn to change my state with kings.

Reply

"Hark, hark, the lark at heav'n's gate sings, and
 Phoebus"
Will raise a flame while "mary-buds begin
To ope their golden eyes." An olden rebus
Of blooming emblems opened up, within

Which ever-ready treasure we will find
A wealth of calm ascending in our heart,
That quiets the ungentle, jealous mind
By hope of morning star. A tear may start...

By memory refreshed, the inward eye,
Transcending self, in welcome solitude
Embowered, feels, the lark and flower nigh,
A welcome health dispel the envy-mood.

    If sulks appall (and some have called them sin)
    Sing Love—alembicate a flame within.

Sonnet 30

When to the sessions of sweet silent thought
I summon up remembrance of things past,
I sigh the lack of many a thing I sought
And with old woes new wail my dear time's waste,

Then can I drown an eye, unus'd to flow,
For precious friends hid in death's dateless night,
And weep afresh love's long since cancell'd woe,
And moan th' expense of many a vanish'd sight:

Then can I grieve at grievances foregone,
And heavily from woe to woe tell o'er
The sad account of fore-bemoaned moan,
Which I new pay as if not paid before.

    But if the while I think on thee, dear friend,
    All losses are restor'd and sorrows end.

Reply

Though there is little we can understand,
That limit need not bound our empathy.
Sad lay for things lamented out of hand
Already we may hear impatiently

And wonder if there be objective cause
For replicated griefs evading reason.
Brain chemistry, like tides, may render laws
Quite clear as guiding every altered season—

Yet rushes of emotion, if by rules
Unknown or known, yet buried deep in things'
Predestination may defy the schools.
The spirit, though, will care. The winds on wings

> Of darkness or of dawn that onward roll,
> Lugubrious, illume—invoke the soul.

Sonnet 31

Thy bosom is endeared with all hearts,
Which I by lacking have supposed dead;
And there reigns Love, and all Love's loving parts,
And all those friends which I thought buried.

How many a holy and obsequious tear
Hath dear religious love stol'n from mine eye
As interest of the dead, which now appear
But things remov'd that hidden in thee lie!

Thou art the grave where buri'd love doth live,
Hung with the trophies of my lovers gone,
Who all their parts of me to thee did give;
That due of many now is thine alone:

> Their images I lov'd I view in thee,
> And thou—all they—hast all the all of me.

Reply

A danger-laden state indeed. Thought dead,
The writer's former comrades prove to be
Directing their assembled love instead
To cynosure of latter amity.

A jealous ire is muffled lightning-fast—
A clever tactic, but we see a catch.
"You're loved by all my friends, so you've surpassed
Poor me so much the more, who cannot match

The merits that would make one worthy of
Their several attentions, nor will I
Gain likelier too-long-alluring love,
Who all my rivals must behold nearby."

    It looks at first like worship—then the flood
    Of ripe resentment riles with bile the blood.

Sonnet 32

If thou survive my well-contented day
When that churl Death my bones with dust shall
    cover
And shalt by fortune once more re-survey
These poor rude lines of thy deceased lover,

Compare them with the bett'ring of the time,
And though they be outstripp'd by every pen,
Reserve them for my love, not for their rhyme,
Exceeded by the height of happier men.

O then vouchsafe me but this loving thought:
'Had my friend's Muse grown with this growing age,
A dearer birth than this his love had brought
To march in ranks of better equipage;

    But since he died and poets better prove,
    Theirs for their style I'll read, his for his love.'

Reply

Though derogating one's ability
To write what's fine and so will suit the friend
Who'd merit lines of treasured memory
More bright than angel follows well the trend

That Petrarch set and Philip Sidney, too,
It signals, here again, despondency
Combined with carping at one's art anew.
I doubt the poet thought indeed that he

Would not keep up with verse's upward flight.
The fancy's rather "At my funeral
(Envisioned gladly) tears would bring to sight
Remembrance that of love my heart was full."—

    A sighing dream that every child has had,
    With heedless people viewed as newly sad.

Sonnet 33

𝔍ull many a glorious morning have I seen
Flatter the mountain tops with sov'reign eye,
Kissing with golden face the meadows green,
Gilding pale streams with heav'nly alchemy,

Anon permit the basest clouds to ride
With ugly rack on his celestial face,
And from the fórlorn world his visage hide,
Stealing unseen to west with this disgrace:

Ev'n so my sun one early morn did shine
With all triumphant splendour on my brow;
But out! alack! he was but one hour mine,
The region cloud hath mask'd him from me now.

    Yet him for this my love no whit disdaineth;
    Suns of the world may stain when heav'n's sun
       staineth.

Reply

Above the solar form the cloudstreams go:
It rides in flaming car athwart the sky.
Come darkling afternoon, dimmed Phoebus' glow
Need trouble no adorer such as I.

The more unlikely to require a sigh:
Gold-mind Apollo governing our lines
In sunray strummed by virtue of the high
Heliacal, inspiring like designs.

Upon the earth, below the moon are suns
Enkindling similarly rhythmed songs.
As each along the guided lifeline runs
To them our pleasure, with our praise, belongs.

    "Ev'n as below," cried Hermes, "so above"—
    Great thrice: in hymn, in wisdom, and in love.

Sonnet 34

Why didst thou promise such a beauteous day
And make me travel forth without my cloak,
To let base clouds o'ertake me in my way,
Hiding thy bravery in their rotten smoke?

'Tis not enough that through the cloud thou break,
To dry the rain on my storm-beaten face,
For no man well of such a salve can speak
That heals the wound and cures not the disgrace—

Nor can thy shame give physic to my grief;
Though thou repent, yet I have still the loss.
Th' offender's sorrow lends but weak relief
To him that bears the strong offence's cross.

    Ah! but those tears are pearl which thy love sheds,
    And they are rich and ransom all ill deeds.

Reply

The dew, sweet tears of Helios' gilded eye,
And as the weeping of a guilty Jove,
Like waters blessed of a pledge might lie
That high attentions may no longer rove

Which, having strayed, their purity had smudged
And covered with a cloak beseeming shame.
These pardoning, the poet hasn't judged
Too hard, nor will continue fixing blame.

Instead, claimed Blake in *Book of Thel*, the dew
That dawn will marry to the waiting grass
One sees with new infusion love bestrew
Descending from the cloud-shapes when they pass.

    Thus friend and writer, reconciled, are one,
    Like pearls of price when melted by the sun.

Sonnet 35

No more be griev'd at that which thou hast done:
Roses have thorns, and silver fountains mud.
Clouds and eclipses stain both moon and sun,
And loathsome canker lives in sweetest bud.

All men make faults, and even I in this,
Authorizing thy trespass with compare,
Myself corrupting, salving thy amiss,
Excusing thy sins more than thy sins are;

For to thy sensual fault I bring in sense—
Thy adverse party is thy advocate—
And 'gainst myself a lawful plea commence:
Such civil war is in my love and hate

> That I an áccessáry needs must be
> To that sweet thief which sourly robs from me.

Reply

Extenuated sentence? Yet the rancor
Is not dismissed. The wild bipolar mind
Continues to be gnawn by crawling canker
Of yet recurring, unrelenting kind.

Judge? Pardoner? Yet now the judge condemns
His act: had he not added laxity
To mercy, furthering offense that stems
From non-commitment found in one not free

Of stormwinds that remorseless in the blood
From dawning swing to darkness, carking care?
Such uncontrol turns greening rush to mud:
'Twill blur distinction, dim the sunlight fair.

    The friend is fickle—but may not be chidden
    By one with eyes undried from winds unbidden.

Sonnet 36

Let me confess that we two must be twain
Although our undivided loves are one:
So shall those blots that do with me remain
Without thy help by me be borne alone.

In our two loves there is but one respect,
Though in our lives a separable spite
Which, though it alter not love's sole effect,
Yet doth it steal sweet hours from love's delight.

I may not evermore acknowledge thee,
Lest my bewailed guilt should do thee shame,
Nor thou with public kindness honour me
Unless thou take that honour from thy name:

> But do not so, I love thee in such sort
> As, thou being mine, mine is thy good report.

Reply

He bears the love-hate that he can't escape
Within himself and, blaming self, would take
The hardest burden that the pure could shape
To charge him with. A sudden couplet-break

May well appear a facile reassurance
That cannot promise to appease a guilt
Or what resentment of the pained endurance
It may entail. The fragile structure built

On careful, care-filled strategy in verse
Attained the balance an equilibrist
Achieves but cannot quite believe in—worse
Will doubt within arise, if he insist.

    A friendship fraught—and yet in wedlock we
    That wobbling tightrope-walking often see.

Sonnet 37

As a decrepit father takes delight
To see his active child do deeds of youth,
So I, made lame by Fortune's dearest spite,
Take all my comfort of thy worth and truth,

For whether beauty, birth, or wealth, or wit,
Or any of these all, or all, or more,
Entitl'd in thy parts do crowned sit,
I make my love engrafted to this store.

So then I am not lame, poor, nor despis'd,
Whilst that this shadow doth such substance give
That I in thy abundance am suffic'd,
And by a part of all thy glory live.

    Look what is best, that best I wish in thee:
    This wish I have, then ten times happy me!

Reply

That shadow, image, or idea by
Whose aid the poet would be comforted
Reminds me rather of the wraiths that fly
About in Hades, phantoms of the dead.

It hasn't any substance of the world
Above—it was of such Achilles claimed:
"Far better be a slave on earth than hurled
In clammy damp and king of shadows named."

For ev'n the "happy me" can make one sad.
Me miserum recall—or "woe is me."
It was in hell itself that Satan had
A chance to moan so long—more lonesome he.

    Sad shade, when cast by plangent wails below
    From joyless Acheron, pales poet-glow.

Sonnet 38

How can my muse want subject to invent
While thou dost breathe, that pour'st into my verse
Thine own sweet argument, too excellent
For every vulgar paper to rehearse?

O give thyself the thanks, if aught in me
Worthy perusal stand against thy sight;
For who's so dumb that cannot write to thee
When thou thyself dost give invention light?

Be thou the tenth Muse, ten times more in worth
Than those old nine which rhymers invocate;
And he that calls on thee, let him bring forth
Eternal numbers to outlive long date.

> If my slight muse do please these curious days,
> The pain be mine, but thine shall be the praise.

Reply

In Plato's writing, Sappho's made the muse
Who merited to be the tenth, and her
When added to the standard ninefold whose
Art-ministry is welcome, I'd prefer

As being goddess while a mortal bard.
If worthy scholiasts will never prove
That Shakespeare knew her, yet it would be hard
To keep the two apart, for in his love

He spoke of "master-mistress." That apart,
He artfully, remarkably, compares
The sovran of his large and lyric heart
To goddess, not a god. And, brave, he dares

    To pray he may attain eternity
    In versing with the aid of such as s/he.

Sonnet 39

O how thy worth with manners may I sing,
When thou art all the better part of me?
What can mine own praise to mine own self bring?
And what is't but mine own when I praise thee?

Even for this, let us divided live,
And our dear love lose name of single one,
That by this separation I may give
That due to thee which thou deserv'st alone.

O absence! what a torment wouldst thou prove
Were it not thy sour leisure gave sweet leave
To entertain the time with thoughts of love,
Which time and thoughts so sweetly doth deceive,

    And that thou teachest how to make one twain
    By praising him here who doth hence remain.

Reply

We well may guess behind a part of this
May lie the opposite of what is said:
The problem isn't that he'd want to miss
The pride his friend's a part of him. Instead,

An ample time apart he will require
To write. Unaltering attendance on
A lover slackens, dampening desire—
Time lost inciting ire that it is gone.

This limit isn't hidden altogether
But surfaces within the latter lines
Inquiring of a friendly absence whether
It might not better suit the scribe-designs.

    Too highly rated aid is come-with-me.
    Withdrawal, authoring are company.

Sonnet 40

Take all my loves, my love, yea take them all:
What hast thou then more than thou hadst before?
No love, my love, that thou mayst true love call;
All mine was thine before thou hadst this more.

Then if for my love thou my love receivest,
I cannot blame thee, for my love thou usest;
But yet be blam'd if thou thyself deceivest
By wilful taste of what thyself refusest.

I do forgive thy robb'ry, gentle thief,
Although thou steal thee all my poverty:
And yet love knows it is a greater grief
To bear love's wrong than hate's known injury.

    Lascivious grace, in whom all ill well shows,
    Kill me with spites, yet we must not be foes.

Reply

He loves the man who loves the ladyfriend
Of whom the poet is enamored, so
Along with conflicts that will never end,
Together yet with enmity will grow

What liking will survive in rivalry.
Beloved friend and bard identify:
The more they love the lady, more they'll be
Each lover mirrored in the other's eye.

We've here a complicated novel-plot,
Or drama deep as any ever writ.
Suspense is building. We'll be watching what
Intriguing wiles will, written, rise from it.

    Love-hate has baited with his lines before:
    We, muddle unabated, wait for more.

Sonnet 41

Those pretty wrongs that liberty commits
When I am sometime absent from thy heart
Thy beauty and thy years full well befits,
For still temptation follows where thou art.

Gentle thou art, and therefore to be won;
Beauteous thou art, therefore to be assail'd;
And when a woman woos, what woman's son
Will sourly leave her till he have prevail'd?

Ay me! but yet thou mightst my seat forbear,
And chide thy beauty and thy straying youth,
Who lead thee in their riot even there
Where thou art forc'd to break a twofold truth,

>Hers by thy beauty tempting her to thee,
>Thine by thy beauty being false to me.

Reply

The more attractive man and woman both
Are found, the more they'll be attracted. This
Would perfect be, but leaves the poet loth
To laud the double object of a bliss

Which will become a bale until he find
A way to reconciliation. He,
Triangularly trapped, must needs unbind
A puzzle-knot in trigonometry.

If this romance were Grecian, one might come
Upon some mitigating strategies:
Kind friends, recalling glad *Symposium*,
Like Diotima seen by Socrates

> Might raise her up in mind to skiey height—
> No rivalry for Lady angel-bright.

Sonnet 42

That thou hast her it is not all my grief,
And yet it may be said I loved her dearly;
That she hath thee is of my wailing chief,
A loss in love that touches me more nearly.

Loving offenders, thus I will excuse ye:
Thou dost love her because thou know'st I love her;
And for my sake ev'n so doth she abuse me,
Suff'ring my friend for my sake to approve her.

If I lose thee, my loss is my love's gain,
And losing her, my friend hath found that loss;
Both find each other, and I lose both twain,
And both for my sake lay on me this cross.

    But here's the joy: my friend and I are one.
    Sweet flatt'ry! then she loves but me alone.

Reply

We've known how well the troubled suitor tries
To prove true Love and Logos are but one.
But loving, paradoxical, defies
Our reason—both are speedily undone.

I learned a theorem: two items equal
To *one* thing thus are equal to each *other*.
Two friends of mine, though, in a stifling sequel,
Lost love in overwhelming null would smother.

It is a fond illusion to suppose
That enthymeme or sweet sophrosynë
Might yet compete successfully with those
Desires and enmities we feel and see.

    Emotions read no plain geometries
    Nor duly credit any Q.E.D.'s.

Sonnet 43

When most I wink, then do mine eyes best see,
For all the day they view things unrespected;
But when I sleep, in dreams they look on thee
And, darkly bright, are bright in dark directed.

Then thou, whose shadow shadows doth make
    bright,
How would thy shadow's form form happy show
To the clear day with thy much clearer light
When to unseeing eyes thy shade shines so!

How would, I say, mine eyes be blessed made
By looking on thee in the living day
When in dead night thy fair imperfect shade
Through heavy sleep on sightless eyes doth stay!

    All days are nights to see till I see thee,
    And nights bright days when dreams do show
        thee me.

Reply

The poet made this antic shape display
Chiasmal acrobatic rhetoric:
Reversals mirrored prink, parade, and play,
But alter not the calming wizard trick

Of what I'd call syntactic metaphor:
"Dark-bright, bright-dark"—the pattern of the game,
Symmetrical, harmonious—the lore
It means to teach, and so with grace to tame

The lurking opposition that awakes
When dreaming's made the darker mind aware
Of martyrdoms-in-waiting. Fancy fakes
A fonder charmer's art to quell them there...

    The envy seen too frequently before,
    Coils loosed, will never fool: we joy no more.

Sonnet 44

If the dull substance of my flesh were thought,
Injurious distance should not stop my way;
For then, despite of space, I would be brought
From limits far remote, where thou dost stay.

No matter then although my foot did stand
Upon the farthest earth remov'd from thee,
For nimble thought can jump both sea and land
As soon as think the place where he would be.

But, ah! thought kills me that I am not thought,
To leap large lengths of miles when thou art gone,
But that, so much of earth and water wrought,
I must attend time's leisure with my moan,

    Receiving nought by elements so slow
    But heavy tears, badges of either's woe.

Reply

Our tears are heavy, wet, recalling mud,
And emblemize an earth-and-water weight,
Brute matter állied, by our flesh and blood,
To crude, unmoving bulk, a sluggard state.

In Mudburg, or Bouville, a Frenchman felt
Depression sketched in Sartre's *La nausée:*
His too, too solid flesh would never melt,
Unsullied, or evaporate—but stay:

It is the dream of one who's not at home
But feels the deepest need to get away.
A rooted being might be loth to roam
And glad to make a sculpture out of clay:

> Egyptian, Hebrew potter-godlings can
> In statue-garden craft an artful Man.

Sonnet 45

The other two, slight air and purging fire,
Are both with thee wherever I abide;
The first my thought, the other my desire,
These present-absent with swift motion slide.

For when these quicker elements are gone
In tender embassy of love to thee,
My life, being made of four, with two alone
Sinks down to death, oppress'd with melanch'ly,

Until life's composition be recur'd
By those swift messengers return'd from thee,
Who ev'n but now come back again, assur'd
Of thy fair health, recounting it to me.

    This told, I joy; but then, no longer glad,
    I send them back again and straight grow sad.

Reply

𝔍f air and fire, most flying and most free,
Bear thought and passion on their wings away,
They lead us not to new security
But, fickle in their nature, never stay.

Who therefore some stability would find
Had better supplement his love with art:
The existential future neither mind
Will comfort nor the being-seeking heart.

Swift process and the "flow" of Heraclitus,
Which is a river and a riving fire,
Twin emblem of Becoming, will invite us
To know that neither knowledge nor desire

> May find fit object whereupon to nest:
> The mind is tireless, climbing Neverrest.

Sonnet 46

Mine eye and heart are at a mortal war
How to divide the conquest of thy sight;
Mine eye my heart thy picture's sight would bar,
My heart mine eye the freedom of that right.

My heart doth plead that thou in him dost lie—
A closet never pierc'd with crystal eyes—
But the defendant doth that plea deny,
And says in him thy fair appearance lies.

To 'cide this title is impanelled
A quest of thoughts, all tenants to the heart,
And by their verdict is determined
The clear eye's moiety and the dear heart's part,

> As thus: mine eye's due is thy outward part,
> And my heart's right thy inward love of heart.

Reply

So heart and eye have fought since ancient times.
Our inner life won't trust the outward "show."
In German, "Schein" means "shine" and "seem."
    What rhymes
May link essential and apparent glow?

In Aristotle, little conflict we
Perceive between the form of worthy being
And its inherent growth-entelechy:
What's healthy is within, plus what we're seeing.

But Plato mere appearance would deride:
External shapes are copies, he would claim,
Of higher Forms that in some heaven hide—
Sublunar kinds degraded, not the same

    Except that they are kindred in the spirit
    That kens the Truth, if barely coming near it.

Sonnet 47

Betwixt mine eye and heart a league is took,
And each doth good turns now unto the other.
When that mine eye is famish'd for a look
Or heart in love with sighs himself doth smother,

With my love's picture then my eye doth feast
And to the painted banquet bids my heart;
Another time mine eye is my heart's guest
And in his thoughts of love doth share a part.

So, either by thy picture or my love,
Thyself away art present still with me;
For thou no farther than my thoughts canst move,
And I am still with them, and they with thee;

> Or, if they sleep, thy picture in my sight
> Awakes my heart, to heart's and eye's delight.

Reply

An ontologic marriage of the two
Is reachable and easy if we want—
Internal essence and external view
Conflictual advantage needn't vaunt.

The active intellect (Platonic soul),
Plotinus would, conciliating, state,
As one with Mind enlivening the Whole,
Man's form with ray sublime will animate.

Platonic Form, we learn, no longer hides
In high immortal realms and far away
But rather in the earthly mind abides
And shines. We, cave-awakened, meet the day.

    So, heart and eye, Ficino finds, are one,
    Reborn and Florence-formed in morning sun.

Sonnet 48

How careful was I when I took my way
Each trifle under truest bars to thrust,
That to my use it might unused stay
From hands of falsehood, in sure wards of trust!

But thou, to whom my jewels trifles are,
Most worthy comfort, now my greatest grief,
Thou best of dearest and mine only care
Art left the prey of every vulgar thief.

Thee have I not lock'd up in any chest,
Save where thou art not, though I feel thou art,
Within the gentle closure of my breast,
From whence at pleasure thou mayst come and part;

    And even thence thou wilt be stol'n, I fear,
    For truth proves thievish for a prize so dear.

Reply

As earlier the poet made it clear
We all are formed of earth, air, water, fire,
The cherished friend who deepliest may cheer,
As most replete with what we most admire,

Will be, like all our animated clay,
In large part fire and air, which move, diffuse,
And straying, scorning firmness, wend their sway
Across the far horizon—what we lose

Far less than what we gain, when guaranteed
Are best beloved runner-liberties.
Love, golden, turns to fool's-gold when unfreed—
Quicksilver-light his life as Mercury's.

> Be therefore not enamored of your wealth,
> But grant it amply, for your mental health.

Sonnet 49

Against that time, if ever that time come,
When I shall see thee frown on my defécts,
Whenas thy love hath cast his utmost sum,
Call'd to that audit by advis'd respects;

Against that time when thou shalt strangely pass
And scarcely greet me with that sun, thine eye,
When love, converted from the thing it was,
Shall reasons find of settl'd gravity:

Against that time do I ensconce me here
Within the knowledge of mine own desert
And this my hand against myself uprear
To guard the lawful reasons on thy part.

> To leave poor me thou hast the strength of laws,
> Since why to love I can allege no cause.

Reply

By future threatened, he can build a fence
And not be wounded when abandoned or
Neglected by his friend. He'll less be tense
With lesser expectation. So the more

Disclaimed the merit, slighter is the hope:
He'll not be disillusioned, disabused.
Prepare yourself, that you may better cope
With love's denial if it be refused.

And here Carlyle will note the way to go;
Your gladness: ratio of what you get
In fact to what you had expected, so
While self-denial is a trial, yet

> High hopes mean dole, depression. Flee from thence!
> Your shelter: "Center of Indifference."

Sonnet 50

How heavy do I journey on the way,
When what I seek, my weary travel's end,
Doth teach that ease and that repose to say,
'Thus far the miles are measur'd from thy friend!'

The beast that bears me, tired with my woe,
Plods dully on, to bear that weight in me,
As if by some instinct the wretch did know
His rider lov'd not speed, being made from thee:

The bloody spur can not provoke him on
That sometimes anger thrusts into his hide;
Which heavily he answers with a groan,
More sharp to me than spurring to his side.

> For that same groan doth put this in my mind:
> My grief lies onward and my joy behind.

Reply

𝕴 feel for him, and yet more deeply for
The beast of burden bearing him away.
The more he's peeved the friend is gone, the more
He'll wildly spur the steed that tried to stay,

Appearing to object with stubborn pout.
Yet all dissatisfaction that the man
Will suffer wants an utterance, will out—
The blind unconscious drives him as it can:

"I can't attack my task, my friend, my heart,
My weakness, or my conflict, or my wrath.
So I'll attack the horse, which, for its part,
Would, froward, slow me on my chosen path!"

    A fight can start—we feel a target's needed—
    With arguments of reason quite unheeded.

Sonnet 51

𝕿hus can my love excuse the slow offence
Of my dull bearer when from thee I speed:
From where thou art why should I haste me thence?
Till I return, of posting is no need.

O what excuse will my poor beast then find
When swift extremity can seem but slow?
Then should I spur, though mounted on the wind;
In winged speed no motion shall I know.

Then can no horse with my desire keep pace;
Therefore desire, of perfect'st love being made,
Shall neigh—no dull flesh—in his fiery race;
But love, for love, thus shall excuse my jade:

> 'Since from thee going, he went wilful-slow,
> Towards thee I'll run and give him leave to go.'

Reply

As, when we're melancholy, everything
About conspires to magnify our wrath,
So when we feel delight, as prideful king,
Will nought impair the dashing spirit-path.

Projected anger made the world our foe,
And so, projected happiness, our friend.
Before, all vileness tried to work us woe—
Our present lively bliss will never end.

As we who were the weakest of the weak
Were blasted by the world's almighty ire,
So now, whatever comely goal we seek
Must come our way—we only need aspire.

    A prior worm, a future deity,
    Alike in whimsied vision, fools are we.

Sonnet 52

So am I as the rich, whose blessed key
Can bring him to his sweet up-locked treasure,
The which he will not every hour survey,
For blunting the fine point of seldom pleasure.

Therefore are feasts so solemn and so rare,
Since, seldom coming in that long year set,
Like stones of worth they thinly placed are,
Or captain jewels in the carcanet.

So is the time that keeps you as my chest,
Or as the wardrobe which the robe doth hide,
To make some special instant special-blest
By new unfolding his imprison'd pride.

    Blessed are you whose worthiness gives scope,
    Being had, to triumph; being lack'd, to hope.

Reply

So, too, Spinoza: "All things excellent
Are difficult as rare." It seems untrue.
Yet to psychology the sentiment
May well appear more cogent when we view

The statement in emotion-laden terms:
We more appreciate a thing that's rare,
Appearing more worthwhile. The mind affirms
What heart had whispered, finding wisdom there.

So Shelley had deplored our apathy—
Routine that dulls the hearing, feeling, seeing.
"The film," he said, "familiarity,"
"Conceals from us the wonder of our being."

    And yet the present minute isn't worse
    Than Hour the First of this our pluriverse.

Sonnet 53

What is your substance, whereof are you made,
That millions of strange shadows on you tend?
Since every one hath, every one, one shade,
And you, but one, can every shadow lend.

Describe Adonis, and the counterfeit
Is poorly imitated after you;
On Helen's cheek all art of beauty set,
And you in Grecian tires are painted new:

Speak of the spring, and foison of the year:
The one doth shadow of your beauty show,
The other as your bounty doth appear,
And you in every blessed shape we know.

    In all external grace you have some part,
    But you like none, none you, for constant heart.

Reply

The man appears in every beauteous thing,
For they are made so by the speaker's love,
Whose mood diffuses madly, gladdening
For him all things below, beside, above.

A Helen, an Adonis, in delight
He's deified, Platonic androgyne
Or supernatural hermaphrodite—
With virtue virile—as a female fine.

Hellenic Helen's Troy went up in flame,
And, yes, Adonis, godlike, yearly dies—
Each life we ken, despite what dreamers claim,
Gods' toy, a mere ephemeron that flies.

    We, by euhemerizing, try to gain
    A lasting pantheon, yet strive in vain.

Sonnet 54

O how much more doth beauty beauteous seem
By that sweet ornament which truth doth give.
The rose looks fair, but fairer we it deem
For that sweet odour which doth in it live.

The canker blooms have full as deep a dye
As the perfumed tincture of the roses,
Hang on such thorns, and play as wantonly
When summer's breath their masked buds discloses:

But, for their virtue only is their show,
They live unwoo'd and unrespected fade,
Die to themselves. Sweet roses do not so;
Of their sweet deaths are sweetest odours made.

    And so of you, beauteous and lovely youth,
    When that shall fade, by verse distills your truth.

Reply

A compliment: while dog-rose, being fake
(Devoid of odor), is revealed in death
As inessential—essences we make
Of honest rose beyond the autumn's breath.

And so the friend will flourish in the lines
Composed for him, when he'll in time expire:
We fragrance may inhale from rare designs
Well limned with wanton-playful sonnet-lyre.

And yet were such a lyric made for me,
I'd be two-minded. Lines of twilit gray—
Funereal, if complimentary!
I'm baffled, puzzled—wonder what to say...

    A soul promotion can attractive be—
    Too rapid, though, that immortality.

Sonnet 55

Not marble nor the gilded monuments
Of princes shall outlive this pow'rful rhyme,
But you shall shine more bright in these conténts
Than unswept stone besmear'd with sluttish time.

When wasteful war shall statues overturn
And broils root out the work of masonry,
Nor Mars his sword nor war's quick fire shall burn
The living record of your memory.

'Gainst death and all-oblivious enmity
Shall you pace forth; your praise shall still find room
Ev'n in the eyes of all posterity
That wear this world out to the ending doom.

    So, till the judgement that yourself arise,
    You live in this, and dwell in lovers' eyes.

Reply

More lasting, Horace claimed, than statue-bronze
Would be the monument he had erected.
No priest or prophet, mage or saint or bonze
Might so extend in fame a friend selected

As fond, adoring poet when he'd choose
A soul on whom to lay the laurel wreath
Himself would share. So neither man could lose
Pure perpetuity, the grass beneath.

In death they'll not be severed—David and
His Jonathan—the psalmist would recall.
No statue captures them. In every land
Through memory they stand and cannot fall.

    Though some in final rise may still believe,
    Ambrosial grow in what you will achieve.

Sonnet 56

Sweet love, renew thy force; be it not said
Thy edge should blunter be than appetite,
Which but to-day by feeding is allay'd,
Tomorrow sharpen'd in his former might.

So, love, be thou: although today thou fill
Thy hungry eyes, ev'n till they wink with fulness,
Tomorrow see again, and do not kill
The spirit of love with a perpetual dulness.

Let this sad interim like the ocean be
Which parts the shore where two contracted new
Come daily to the banks, that when they see
Return of love, more blest may be the view;

> Or call it winter, which being full of care,
> Makes summer's welcome thrice more wish'd, more rare.

Reply

Twin spirits water-parted stand on shore
To scan the far horizon for a sail
Arising from the underworld with more
Of seër-glee than words in vain avail

To utter—see the pathos and the glad
Awakening of heat within the heart?—
Alive as if Ulysses after sad
Bewailing now were newly hailed—the art

Of happy likeness never better seen.
Contrást Lord Roland and Sir Leoline,
Whom woeful "dreary sea now flows between,"
Their friendship severed by their own design.

    For wrath can "work like madness in the brain."
    So Coleridge noted—sundered brothers' pain.

Sonnet 57

Being your slave, what should I do but tend
Upon the hours and times of your desire?
I have no precious time at all to spend,
Nor services to do, till you require.

Nor dare I chide the world-without-end hour,
Whilst I, my sov'reign, watch the clock for you,
Nor think the bitterness of absence sour
When you have bid your servant once adieu;

Nor dare I question with my jealous thought
Where you may be, or your affairs suppose,
But, like a sad slave, stay and think of nought
Save, where you are, how happy you make those.

    So true a fool is love that in your will,
    Though you do anything, he thinks no ill.

Reply

Globe Theater, the world, a universe—
And broad, encomiastic thoughts on these
The reader of his drama will rehearse
And hear in sávants' verbal symphonies

In praise of that almighty artist-will,
A fragrant hymn that daily will arise
While for the saint a votive taper still
May flame ascending ever to the skies.

Yet, slave and pawn of love that here we see,
He cannot shake a spear save by command—
His mighty staff long fallen, how can he
But feel unsalved, abandoned, sad, unmanned?

    So William in the world is worried yet,
    Waylaid and wailing, strangely pain-beset.

Sonnet 58

That god forbid, that made me first your slave,
I should in thought control your times of pleasure,
Or at your hand th' account of hours to crave,
Being your vassal, bound to stay your leisure!

O let me suffer, being at your beck,
Th' imprison'd absence of your liberty;
And patience, tame to suff'rance, bide each check
Without accusing you of injury.

Be where you list, your charter is so strong
That you yourself may privilege your time
To what you will; to you it doth belong
Yourself to pardon of self-doing crime.

> I am to wait, though waiting so be hell,
> Not blame your pleasure, be it ill or well.

Reply

The "let me suffer" charter may recall
Uncannily the contract gladly made
In famous modern fictions that appall:
Furred Venus may much-wanted woes unlade

Upon the willing victim, "Gregor" named
In legal-style agreement that might serve
In "Metamorphosis," whose hero, shamed
As craven namesake, yet would never swerve

From craving for a long self-punishment.
Desire may curdle into masochism:
Devoted, holy loving wholly lent
In kindness Will made pine for an abysm.

    Masóch and learner Kafka relished well
    A pleasant purgatory-heaven-hell.

Sonnet 59

If there be nothing new, but that which is
Hath been before, how are our brains beguil'd,
Which, labouring for invention, bear amiss
The second burthen of a former child!

O that recórd could with a backward look
Ev'n of five hundred courses of the sun
Show me your image in some ántique book,
Since mind at first in character was done!

That I might see what the old world could say
To this composed wonder of your frame;
Whe'r we are mended or whe'r better they,
Or whether revolution be the same.

    O sure I am the wits of former days
    To subjects worse have giv'n admiring praise.

Reply

An irony within the final lines:
We well may wonder what the answer proves,
Whatever it might be. The mind resigns,
Unsatisfied, to ponder one it loves.

Then what's the thinking here? I reconstruct:
"Do I pursue a peerless paragon—
Unique in hist'ry? Or should love reluct,
Forsake the futile chase embarked upon?"

He'd like to shame whoever might compare
His idol with a life-form gone before—
Does he not rather beg the brain to dare
Conceive past, future men who'd offer more?

    Recurrence needn't war with form supernal:
    Love moments only: cover's one with kernel.

Sonnet 60

Like as the waves make towards the pebbled shore,
So do our minutes hasten to their end;
Each changing place with that which goes before,
In sequent toil all forwards do contend.

Nativity, once in the main of light,
Crawls to maturity, wherewith being crown'd,
Crooked eclipses 'gainst his glory fight,
And Time that gave doth now his gift confound.

Time doth transfix the flourish set on youth
And delves the parallels in beauty's brow,
Feeds on the rarities of nature's truth,
And nothing stands but for his scythe to mow:

    And yet to times in hope my verse shall stand,
    Praising thy worth despite his cruel hand.

Reply

Three metaphors at strife we may detect:
Our life in time—a sea of sequent waves
That crawl to shore, relentlessly are wrecked,
Yet then revive when ocean, steady, laves.

We, next, are like a sun, or solar light,
Swift-moving through the heaven to our end—
Our might eclipsed, we suffer, yet we fight
Ahead in spite of what the signs portend.

And, third, what digs the wrinkles in our brow
Will keenly, far more harshly, scythe us down—
The art that let our cheeks be carmined now
To reaper's ire will yield of grim renown.

> The last two lines on immortality
> Are trying hard to reconcile the three.

Sonnet 61

Is it thy will thy image should keep open
My heavy eyelids to the weary night?
Dost thou desire my slumbers should be broken
While shadows like to thee do mock my sight?

Is it thy spirit that thou send'st from thee
So far from home into my deeds to pry,
To find out shames and idle hours in me,
The scope and tenure of thy jealousy?

O no! thy love, though much, is not so great:
It is my love that keeps mine eye awake,
Mine own true love that doth my rest defeat
To play the watchman ever for thy sake:

> For thee watch I whilst thou dost wake elsewhere,
> From me far off, with others all too near.

Reply

The watchman holding vigil through the night
Is overseër, "Over-I" of me.
The "inwit," inner, infiltrating light
Would ferret out all fallow laxity.

He may appear in loved and shining shape
Of one I'm trying to idealize:
Yet as I lie, awake, aware, agape,
He's merely mirroring my own bright eyes—

And ev'n if in myself, remaining still
A father-god of skiey jealousy,
Resentful of the lower mind that will
Defy the guiding right of such as he.

    'Tis I who grant these watchmen avid pow'r
    To pry and with a lampad high to lour.

Sonnet 62

Sin of self-love possesseth all mine eye
And all my soul, and all my every part;
And for this sin there is no remedy,
It is so grounded inward in my heart.

Methinks no face so gracious is as mine,
No shape so true, no truth of such account,
And for myself mine own worth do define,
As I all other in all worths surmount.

But when my glass shows me myself indeed
Beated and chapp'd with tann'd antiquity,
Mine own self-love quite cóntrary I read:
Self so self-loving were iniquity.

   'Tis thee, my self, that for myself I praise,
   Painting my age with beauty of thy days.

Reply

In two quite diff'ring ways, I've read this plaint.
When shocking changes time and age had wrought
Upon my body, skin dried, hair lost, taint
Of spot or graying, first occurred the thought:

A clever and instructive way to show
A wise Buddhistic distancing from vain
Excessive beauty-pride—our new-gone glow.
Far-sightedness in elders—well-won gain,

To move the world away as we withdraw...
Yet, here, the poet's youthful! Is it wise
To deprecate himself in humble awe
Of idol-form belov'd, for which he sighs?

    Bemoaned appearance, though it can beseem
    The old, is troubling in a young man's dream.

Sonnet 63

Against my love shall be as I am now,
With Time's injurious hand crush'd and o'erworn;
When hours have drain'd his blood and fill'd his brow
With lines and wrinkles; when his youthful morn

Hath travell'd on to age's steepy night,
And all those beauties whereof now he's king
Are vanishing, or vanish'd out of sight,
Stealing away the treasure of his spring;

For such a time do I now fortify
Against confounding age's cruel knife,
That he shall never cut from memory
My sweet love's beauty, though my lover's life:

> His beauty shall in these black lines be seen,
> And they shall live, and he in them still green.

Reply

The poet, plainly, isn't ancient, so
I ponder on the strange "antiquity"
He said he had and now, foretelling woe,
Imagines for the lover: could it be

That, made aware of failing strategy,
He'd compensate by painting youth as doomed
And art, his own, as blooming youthfully
(Despite what handsome rivals had assumed)?

More dark than night had been his latter mood
And he, it seemed, in snaring lines entrapped,
With none of those rare attributes endued
That ways to lover's favor might have mapped—

> Yet holy hope will spring in greening leaf
> With vernal verse, of gleaming cheer the chief!

Sonnet 64

When I have seen by Time's fell hand defaced
The rich-proud cost of outworn buri'd age;
When sometime lofty tow'rs I see down-razed,
And brass eternal slave to mortal rage;

When I have seen the hungry ocean gain
Advantage on the kingdom of the shore
And the firm soil win of the wat'ry main,
Increasing store with loss, and loss with store;

When I have seen such interchange of state,
Or state itself confounded to decay,
Ruin hath taught me thus to ruminate
That Time will come and take my love away.

    This thought is as a death which cannot choose
    But weep to have that which it fears to lose.

Reply

𝔅ecoming is a coming into being
Along with passing of a thing away.
Though every gift that we're this minute seeing
Evade us after decades, or a day,

To fail and gain must be in this agreeing:
That neither is predestined here to stay.
The autumn leaf that red from green is freeing
Might not be gone tomorrow, though it may.

Each thing is halfway nothing, likewise we.
Uncanny heartlessness? The half of heart.
So death and birth are twinned, comminglingly.
When viewed afar, what seemed to me to part

    Draws near to all whose new teléscopy
    Perspective altered by an easy art.

Sonnet 65

Since brass, nor stone, nor earth, nor boundless
    sea,
But sad mortality o'ersways their power,
How with this rage shall beauty hold a plea,
Whose action is no stronger than a flower?

O how shall summer's honey breath hold out
Against the wrackful siege of batt'ring days
When rocks impregnable are not so stout
Nor gates of steel so strong but Time decays?

O fearful meditation! Where, alack,
Shall Time's best jewel from Time's chest lie hid?
Or what strong hand can hold his swift foot back?
Or who his spoil of beauty can forbid?

    O none, unless this miracle have might,
    That in black ink my love may still shine bright.

Reply

If art should sublimate, or substitute
For life that falls away by what shall rise
In newer body that may better suit,
Wherein no canker of declining lies,

Can it then brag of living unity?
The sprightly human form in youthful beauty
Has the appealing gift of symmetry,
Which to approximate would be art's duty.

To state, develop, then to theme return—
The three-part structure of sonata-form.
Plot-twine the conflict, then untying earn
A balance for the classic drama's norm.

> But twelve lines' riddle, then the insight, quick?
> Let's find the symmetry within this trick...

Sonnet 66

Tir'd with all these, for restful death I cry,
As to behold desért a beggar born,
And needy nothing trimm'd in jollity,
And purest faith unhappily forsworn,

And gilded honour shamefully misplac'd,
And maiden virtue rudely strumpeted,
And right perfection wrongfully disgrac'd,
And strength by limping sway disabled,

And art made tongue-tied by authority,
And folly—doctor-like—controlling skill,
And simple truth miscall'd simplicity,
And captive good attending captain ill:

>   Tir'd with all these, from these would I be gone,
>   Save that, to die, I leave my love alone.

Reply

To leave a reader never ill at ease,
The query in my former poem posed
I'll answer: there are many symmetries
In any Shakespeare lines, however glozed.

The anaphoric chanting with the "and"
Has lulled with balanced, crafted melody.
The next-to-last, chiasmal line will stand
For supplemental micro-symmetry.

But other beauties than symmetric wait:
The building up to couplet thoughtfully
Beyond long pondering can emulate
The lovely structure of discovery.

    Refind the sweet "eureka!" many times
    And symmetries appear, as in the rhymes.

Sonnet 67

Ah! wherefore with infection should he live
And with his presence grace impiety,
That sin by him advantage should achieve
And lace itself with his society?

Why should false painting imitate his cheek
And steal dead seeming of his living hue?
Why should poor beauty indirectly seek
Roses of shadow, since his rose is true?

Why should he live, now Nature bankrupt is,
Beggar'd of blood to blush through lively veins?
For she hath no exchequer now but his
And, proud of many, lives upon his gains.

> O him she stores, to show what wealth she had
> In days long since, before these last so bad.

Reply

The friend proved so much better than the rest
Of nature and dirempt society,
He has become the measure and the test
Of what is lesser than resplendent he,

Who's mainly kept alive that we may know
Or vaguely guess at former times' perfection.
Past dew-pearl hours were better: most things go
To ruin fast, in wretched misdirection.

Our childhood we idealize, in search
Of simpler and more happy olden days.
Unlucky, left in grave historic lurch,
We find faint comfort in those golden ways—

    All Edens being paradises lost,
    And paragons long fallen, to our cost.

Sonnet 68

Thus is his cheek the map of days outworn,
When beauty liv'd and died as flow'rs do now,
Before these bastard signs of fair were born,
Or durst inhabit on a living brow;

Before the golden tresses of the dead,
The right of sepulchres, were shorn away
To live a second life on second head;
Ere beauty's dead fleece made another gay.

In him those holy antique hours are seen
Without all ornament, itself and true,
Making no summer of another's green,
Robbing no old to dress his beauty new;

> And him as for a map doth Nature store
> To show false Art what beauty was of yore.

Reply

The theme of deep nostalgia newly broached
Has proved attractive, as it ever will.
Have disappointments, loaded on, encroached
On every boldened joy? Reach Eden still

Within the gladsome past no dread besets.
Greek Hesiod, Rome's Ovid show the fall
That Milton, torn and Bible-worn, regrets.
Gold, silver, bronze, and iron (worst of all)…

"Seek shelter in the comfort of the tomb,"
Poor Shelley counseled, in divine despair.
Psychologists would claim he meant the womb
Though of this hidden rhyming unaware.

> The "Other" or the "little object o"
> Is love-dream sought in vague Lacanian woe.

Sonnet 69

Those parts of thee that the world's eye doth view
Want nothing that the thought of hearts can mend;
All tongues—the voice of souls—give thee that due,
Utt'ring bare truth, ev'n so as foes commend.

Thy outward thus with outward praise is crown'd;
But those same tongues that give thee so thine own
In other accents do this praise confound
By seeing farther than the eye hath shown.

They look into the beauty of thy mind,
And that in guess they measure by thy deeds;
Then—churls—their thoughts, although their eyes
        were kind,
To thy fair flow'r add the rank smell of weeds:

> But why thy odour matcheth not thy show,
> The soil is this, that thou dost common grow.

Reply

We know not whether there are data that
Confirm the hasty charges of the churls:
High-floating praise we've heard, though, might go flat
If smiling words and acts weren't perfect pearls.

Encomiastic rhapsody reveals
What insecurities are compensated
While over soul bereaved there slowly steals
A doubt well-grounded if a bit belated.

The more the prayers, hope, invested in
The object of one's love, once deified,
Proportionally great's the graver sin:
To show our deep ideal must be denied.

> Be censured if your life can't justify
> The scented essence that you sent on high.

Sonnet 70

That thou art blam'd shall not be thy deféct,
For slander's mark was ever yet the fair;
The ornament of beauty is suspéct,
A crow that flies in heaven's sweetest air.

So thou be good, slander doth but approve
Thy worth the greater, being woo'd of time;
For canker vice the sweetest buds doth love,
And thou present'st a pure unstained prime.

Thou hast pass'd by the ambush of young days
Either not assail'd, or victor being charg'd;
Yet this thy praise can not be so thy praise
To tie up envy, evermore enlarg'd.

> If some suspéct of ill mask'd not thy show,
> Then thou alone kingdoms of hearts shouldst owe.

Reply

We all need validation, so if one
You value cause a daunting disabusal,
His image rescue, lest you be undone
By gloomy sequel of your love's refusal.

In flattery-reproof-repentance trains
Of mood we hearken to, our hearts engage:
We learn to deal with sharp suspicion-pains
To purge the bubble-burst that may enrage.

Intensive labor are the acts of wrath—
They drain away what flame will keep us young:
Tranquillity would rather tread the path
Of peace, where praises featly may be sung.

>The Tree of Life is love. The other Tree
>Is loved when we partake—but tastefully.

Sonnet 71

No longer mourn for me when I am dead
Than you shall hear the surly sullen bell
Give warning to the world that I am fled
From this vile world with vilest worms to dwell:

Nay, if you read this line, remember not
The hand that writ it, for I love you so
That I in your sweet thoughts would be forgot
If thinking on me then should make you woe.

O if, I say, you look upon this verse
When I perhaps compounded am with clay,
Do not so much as my poor name rehearse,
But let your love ev'n with my life decay,

> Lest the wise world should look into your moan
> And mock you with me after I am gone.

Reply

Vile world, vile worms, our life is death, and worse
For leading to a netherworld of clay,
Yet like a violin, the sighing verse,
Revealing more than ever word can say,

Will please by having sung, for numbers charm
The soul from out the body, we are taught,
And higher than the moon, immune to harm,
Possess a realm by only rhythm raught.

Archaic is the diction of my hymn,
For I would bear you to an ancient age,
The legacy in melody relimn
Of one congenial music-maker mage:

>Pythagorean "All is number." We
>May humbly feel that sphery theme will free.

Sonnet 72

O lest the world should task you to recite
What merit lived in me, that you should love
After my death, dear love, forget me quite,
For you in me can nothing worthy prove

Unless you would devise some virtuous lie
To do more for me than mine own desert,
And hang more praise upon deceased I
Than niggard truth would willingly impart.

O lest your true love may seem false in this,
That you for love speak well of me untrue,
My name be buri'd where my body is,
And live no more to shame nor me nor you.

> For I am sham'd by that which I bring forth,
> And so should you, to love things nothing worth.

Reply

As poet or as actor, playwright, he
Assumes he will but little be esteemed.
How overpowering an irony
That now he overtowers all we've dreamed.

Indeed I'd thought the classic poets were
As people of another species, far
Beyond the mediocre that occur
On earth—look down as from a brilliant star.

Three decades had I lectured on the "greats"
Before the rending thought came home to me
That everything they wrote anticipates
What we ourselves can make of melody.

> Who thought himself quite low was brought so high
> You reckoned not he'd beckon from the sky.

Sonnet 73

That time of year thou mayst in me behold
When yellow leaves, or none, or few, do hang
Upon those boughs which shake against the cold,
Bare ruin'd choirs, where late the sweet birds sang.

In me thou see'st the twilight of such day
As after sunset fadeth in the west,
Which by and by black night doth take away,
Death's second self, that seals up all in rest.

In me thou see'st the glowing of such fire
That on the ashes of his youth doth lie
As the death-bed whereon it must expire,
Consum'd with that which it was nourish'd by.

> This thou perceiv'st, which makes thy love more strong,
> To love that well which thou must leave ere long.

Reply

My sanguine personality requires,
Each time I read a poet's plaint, that I
Seek out, mid ash-choked and expiring fires,
A lesson lighter than an anguished cry.

We find invoked the phoenix-rising myth
Of resurrection over centuries:
So will the flame the sayer started with
In play and lyric hymn revive with ease.

A subtext brings the reader a reward.
Detect, reveal, beneath its covering,
Banked fire that, saved for later, will afford
Preságed accession of the magian king:

> Let's pry between the lines, behind the letters,
> To seek whatever find our quest-life betters.

Sonnet 74

But be contented: when that fell arrest
Without all bail shall carry me away,
My life hath in this line some interest,
Which for memorial still with thee shall stay.

When thou reviewest this, thou dost review
The very part was consecrate to thee:
The earth can have but earth, which is his due;
My spirit is thine, the better part of me.

So then thou hast but lost the dregs of life,
The prey of worms, my body being dead,
The coward conquest of a wretch's knife,
Too base of thee to be remembered.

    The worth of that is that which it contains,
    And that is this, and this with thee remains.

Reply

I learned from Goethe: monuments for them
Are little needed who have built their own.
They've no necessity of diadem
Whose legacy outshines the em'rald stone.

Memorial may those endeavors be
Whereinto avidly a radiance poured.
The "life-blood of a master-spirit" we
May judge the work of such post-mortal lord

(So Milton), "treasured up" for life beyond.
And immortality can be increased
If we, with reverence far more than fond,
Ensure their writing-scions won't have ceased.

    The blood-line of the blessed never dies
    While shines the light in lyric-children's eyes.

Sonnet 75

So are you to my thoughts as food to life
Or as sweet-season'd show'rs are to the ground;
And for the peace of you I hold such strife
As 'twixt a miser and his wealth is found:

Now proud as an enjoyer, and anon
Doubting the filching age will steal his treasure;
Now counting best to be with you alone,
Then better'd that the world may see my pleasure;

Sometime all full with feasting on your sight,
And by and by clean starved for a look;
Possessing or pursuing no delight
Save what is had or must from you be took.

    Thus do I pine and surfeit day by day,
    Or gluttoning on all, or all away.

Reply

𝔉rom loneliness—to friends; then—coming back:
Life drives to art, then art again to life.
A surfeit growing from initial lack
Is purged in motion pendular. No strife

Awaits the oscillation if it go
In patterned manner and predictably.
A movement's better moderate and slow,
Lest conflict rise, and heart's-love harmed should be.

Yet writers cannot always harmonize
The needs for loneliness and for a friend.
To see the daimon with his fiery eyes,
To hear the melody the muses lend,

    To go to heaven, meek nepheliad,
    I pendulums forget, in glow am glad.

Sonnet 76

Why is my verse so barren of new pride,
So far from variation or quick change?
Why with the time do I not glance aside
To new-found methods, and to compounds strange?

Why write I still all one, ever the same,
And keep invention in a noted weed,
That every word doth almost tell my name,
Showing their birth, and where they did proceed?

O know, sweet love, I always write of you,
And you and love are still my argument;
So all my best is dressing old words new,
Spending again what is already spent:

    For as the sun is daily new and old,
    So is my love still telling what is told.

Reply

Obsession draws an author, willingly
To circle round a demon-dream-ideal.
So Tennyson in each epiphany
An awe-ful dawn-rose offered, and a wheel.

Red-yellow flame-bloom Pater, dying bird.
Relentlessness I readily expect:
Repetitive, what one has viewed and heard.
But, in the work of Will, can one detect

A central spell? The tenor of the plays
Appeared to frame a huge diversity
Enchanting all from careless youthful days
To latest age—with grand resiliency.

> How comes it that in lyric he'd unloosed
> Persévérative moods prelúding Proust?

Sonnet 77

Thy glass will show thee how thy beauties wear,
Thy dial how thy precious minutes waste;
These vacant leaves thy mind's imprint will bear,
And of this book, this learning mayst thou taste.

The wrinkles which thy glass will truly show
Of mouthed graves will give thee memory;
Thou by thy dial's shady stealth mayst know
Time's thievish progress to eternity.

Look! what thy memory can not contain,
Commit to these waste blanks, and thou shalt find
Those children nurs'd, deliver'd from thy brain,
To take a new acquaintance of thy mind.

    These offices, so oft as thou wilt look,
      Shall profit thee and much enrich thy book.

Reply

𝔉ine white-paged notebook—brighter-screened
    computer—
No present better—pleasantly designed
To whisk off dusty summoning, dull muter
Of Hippocrene, sweet rill where I refined

A tonal skill to mirror fleeting mood,
Reflect in the limpidity of spring
Each impulse-gift by which I am endued
As living human violin to sing.

Then couple gleaming impulse with the will
To penetrate all gloom with glory-spear
And shake off apathy that would instill
A crippling inanition. Let appear

    On blank yet pure-alluring clarity
    Sweet-anthemed, motley-hued, the charact'ry.

Sonnet 78

So oft have I invok'd thee for my Muse
And found such fair assistance in my verse
As every alien pen hath got my use
And under thee their poesy disperse.

Thine eyes, that taught the dumb on high to sing
And heavy ignorance aloft to fly,
Have added feathers to the learned's wing
And given grace a double majesty.

Yet be most proud of that which I compile,
Whose influence is thine and born of thee.
In others' works thou dost but mend the style,
And arts with thy sweet graces graced be;

    But thou art all my art and dost advance
    As high as learning my rude ignorance.

Reply

𝔐y friend, wise Will, is all my art as well:
The part within that seems not wholly me,
That aids me daily more than I can tell,
My pegasean spur supernally.

While mind the mirror black of night descries
(Of hidden love the darkling raven-sun),
The mother-angel-muse her starry eyes
To heart has darted till the writing's done.

Muhammad on Buraq, a lightning steed,
Viewed every mental heaven he had dreamed:
So, too, I scrutinize a skiey screed
And am quite other than I sometime seemed.

> To "bear beyond"—that's meta-phor. So we
> "Outside" the I will "stand"—in ec-stasy.

Sonnet 79

Whilst I alone did call upon thy aid,
My verse alone had all thy gentle grace;
But now my gracious numbers are decay'd,
And my sick Muse doth give another place.

I grant, sweet love, thy lovely argument
Deserves the trávail of a worthier pen;
Yet what of thee thy poet doth invent
He robs thee of, and pays it thee again.

He lends thee virtue, and he stole that word
From thy behaviour; beauty doth he give
And found it in thy cheek: he can afford
No praise to thee but what in thee doth live.

> Then thank him not for that which he doth say,
> Since what he owes thee, thou thyself dost pay.

Reply

Discouragement is double: first, the lines
He wrote today are worse than those before.
And next, the finest of his bright designs
Show forth in noble paradigm far more.

The early poems had appeared to grant
The friend was furtherer of worthy work.
But now the fiery former hierophant
Is worried, and perturbed. Fell demons lurk

Within this labile wail. It is the green
Of envy of a rival, we will learn,
That, entering one's lyrical demesne,
Will verdure wither, verve to earth will turn.

>   I'll friend revere of whom I'd rival be:
>   What envy weakens we too late may see.

Sonnet 80

O how I faint when I of you do write,
Knowing a better spirit doth use your name
And in the praise thereof spends all his might,
To make me tongue-ti'd speaking of your fame!

But since your worth, wide as the ocean is,
The humble as the proudest sail doth bear,
My saucy bark, inferior far to his,
On your broad main doth wilfully appear.

Your shallowest help will hold me up afloat
Whilst he upon your soundless deep doth ride;
Or, being wrack'd, I am a worthless boat,
He of tall building and of goodly pride.

    Then if he thrive and I be cast away,
    The worst was this: my love was my decay.

Reply

The ocean has no favorite, and so
If that distracted friend be likened to
Abysmal deeps marine, the greater woe
For poet on the vaster blank of blue.

Yet may the simile propitiate:
Neptunian master of the wavy realm,
Resplendent-made, can favor with a late
Yet welcome token him that mans the helm

Of boat made vulnerable, subject to
A wound, our weal depending all upon
Grace lent or scanted. Answers may be few
When our bewailed abscondent god is gone.

    Hope unrequited barely can abide
    (Lone, yearning sigh!) the turning of the tide.

Sonnet 81

Or I shall live your epitaph to make,
Or you survive when I in earth am rotten;
From hence your memory death cannot take,
Although in me each part will be forgotten.

Your name from hence immortal life shall have,
Though I, once gone, to all the world must die:
The earth can yield me but a common grave
When you entombed in men's eyes shall lie.

Your monument shall be my gentle verse,
Which eyes not yet created shall o'er-read;
And tongues to be your being shall rehearse,
When all the breathers of this world are dead.

>   You still shall live—such virtue hath my pen—
>   Where breath most breathes, ev'n in the mouths of men.

Reply

What breathing's deepest in the lungs of men?
To feel with spirit filled will mean to be
Essential breath, respiring deeply when
Inspired, as Adam-clay, by deity.

Though altered sounds may halt frail poetry,
The vast, unsoundable, at last lives on.
The ears are few that hear thalassally
Polyphloisboic Homer. Yet though gone

Be Periclean Athens' understanding
Of odes that in a dialectal Greek
Euripides composed, fate countermanding,
The spirit of the plays they find that seek.

    If you would matter long, write mindfully:
    Inscribe in valiant song your odyssey.

Sonnet 82

I grant thou wert not marri'd to my Muse
And therefore mayst without attaint o'erlook
The dedicated words which writers use
Of their fair subject, blessing every book.

Thou art as fair in knowledge as in hue,
Finding thy worth a limit past my praise,
And therefore art enforc'd to seek anew
Some fresher stamp of the time-bett'ring days.

And do so, love; yet when they have devis'd
What strained touches rhetoric can lend,
Thou, truly fair, wert truly sympathiz'd
In true plain words by thy true-telling friend;

> And their gross painting might be better us'd
> Where cheeks need blood: in thee it is abus'd.

Reply

Though cosmic be the scope of reference
(Wide glory in his more-than-amity)
The poet has deployed, in his defense,
The order it explores, and candidly,

Of ever-new connection weathers well
The press for what is novel. Mere cosmetic
Repair would be impediment—to tell
What nature told far better—antithetic

Precisely to our love of wild surprise.
For pluriversal plenitude ensures
That actuality will widen eyes
And not what, trend-engendered, tired, allures.

    If cosmos be with battle-chaos mixed,
    The more elated we, the more transfixed.

Sonnet 83

𝕴 never saw that you did painting need,
And therefore to your fair no painting set;
I found, or thought I found, you did exceed
That barren tender of a poet's debt;

And therefore have I slept in your report,
That you yourself, being éxtant, well might show
How far a modern quill doth come too short,
Speaking of worth, what worth in you doth grow.

This silence for my sin you did impute,
Which shall be most my glory, being dumb;
For I impair not beauty, being mute,
When others would give life, and bring a tomb.

    There lives more life in one of your fair eyes
    Than both your poets can in praise devise.

Reply

Ineffable, unspeakable—good, bad.
Of silence multiple may be the root
When scared or sullen, thunderstruck or sad:
Both dust and ultimates may render mute.

And puzzlement—for how can rivalry
For the solicitude of one much praised
Be proper grievance to complain of, be
A topic by the self-respecting raised?

And then we have the added paradox
That he who had inscribed the man's desert
In manner indefatigable balks
At writing here of tender feelings hurt—

> By morbid theme he's torn of battered "me"
> And forced to have recóurse to flattery.

Sonnet 84

Who is it that says most which can say more
Than this rich praise, that you alone are you?
In whose confine immured is the store
Which should example where your equal grew?

Lean penury within that pen doth dwell
That to his subject lends not some small glory;
But he that writes of you, if he can tell
That you are you, so dignifies his story.

Let him but copy what in you is writ,
Not making worse what nature made so clear,
And such a counterpart shall fame his wit,
Making his style admired everywhere.

> You to your beauteous blessings add a curse,
> Being fond on praise, which makes your praises worse.

Reply

That "fond on" means "a fool for" let us note,
Ev'n as "infatuation," don't forget,
Is being "foolish," "fatuous." To dote
On one's beloved idol or to set

Oneself too high is not the problem here
But having so regrettably forgone
The use of prudence, holding all too dear
Laudations far too heavily laid on

In ministrations by a rival bard!
Good Will would rather give true gratitude.
More sharp than tooth of serpent, and too hard,
This fawning on another, rich but rude.

> Be man or damsel, rather might you flee
> The trials of triangularity.

Sonnet 85

My tongue-ti'd Muse in manners holds her still,
While comments of your praise, richly compil'd,
Reserve their character with golden quill
And precious phrase by all the Muses fil'd.

I think good thoughts, whilst others write good
    words
And like unletter'd clerk still cry 'Amen'
To every hymn that able spirit affords
In polish'd form of well-refined pen.

Hearing you prais'd, I say ''Tis so, 'tis true,'
And to the most of praise add something more;
But that is in my thought, whose love to you,
Though words come hindmost, holds his rank
    before.

    Then others for the breath of words respect,
    Me for my dumb thoughts, speaking in effect.

Reply

The topic widens, for we all have known
The strength of silence in conveying more
Than meager things which could be heard or shown
To utter forth an inner spirit-store.

One word may quite outvie a thousand pictures,
One silence, million words. The fifteenth line
Unspoken, freed from binding verbal strictures,
Will, rounding, crown a sonnet—high design.

The poet Tyutchev, by this view empowered,
Proclaimed, "The thought, once uttered, is a lie."
One feels the phrase with depth divinely dowered,
Though his and William's gift it might defy.

    A holy, ringing silence will invoke
    The poet-lyre by what it, singing, spoke.

Sonnet 86

Was it the proud full sail of his great verse
Bound for the prize of all too precious you
That did my ripe thoughts in my brain inhearse,
Making their tomb the womb wherein they grew?

Was it his spirit, by spirits taught to write
Above a mortal pitch, that struck me dead?
No, neither he nor his compeers by night
Giving him aid my verse astonished.

He, nor that affable familiar ghost
Which nightly gulls him with intelligence
As victors of my silence cannot boast;
I was not sick of any fear from thence,

> But when your countenance fill'd up his line,
> Then lacked I matter: that enfeebl'd mine.

Reply

𝔉rom neediness can we of early days,
Beleaguering, increasing, not escape.
A baby, mirrored in the warming rays
Of mother's fonder eye, adoring shape

Will glimpse and, hungry miser, hoard that wealth,
Which yet when lessened in extended time
Will evermore be longed for, lest the health
Of mind be vanished that will whisper, "I'm

Held dear by one I value: dó not turn
Away the sign of an approving mind
Or I may not, in truth, be moved to yearn
To see and sing, my heart made mute and blind."

    Remaining gracefully, in ranging ways,
    The parent gazing, unapparent, stays.

Sonnet 87

𝔉arewell! thou art too dear for my possessing,
And like enough thou know'st thy estimate.
The charter of thy worth gives thee releasing;
My bonds in thee are all determinate.

For how do I hold thee but by thy granting?
And for that riches where is my deserving?
The cause of this fair gift in me is wanting,
And so my patent back again is swerving.

Thy self thou gav'st, thy own worth then not
    knowing,
Or me to whom thou gav'st it, else mistaking;
So thy great gift, upon misprision growing,
Comes home again, on better judgement making.

    Thus have I had thee as a dream doth flatter,
    In sleep a king, but waking no such matter.

Reply

Investment, capital, terms, contract, worth,
Rights, property, net profit and provisions,
Gifts, riches, and foreclosure, loss and dearth,
Financial calculations and rescissions,

The guides of banking and of charters, grants,
For metaphors of friendship can't be best.
Emotions grow, subside, or, slow, advance,
Antipathetic ever to the test

Of strict contractual mentality
With stipulations and with payment dates
(I owe you this, and that you owe to me):
The language is gratuitous. It grates.

    And so we switch to images of dream
    That friendship-freedom better will beseem.

Sonnet 88

When thou shalt be dispos'd to set me light
And place my merit in the eye of scorn,
Upon thy side against myself I'll fight
And prove thee virtuous though thou art forsworn.

With mine own weakness being best acquainted,
Upon thy part I can set down a story
Of faults conceal'd wherein I am attainted,
That thou in losing me shalt win much glory,

And I by this will be a gainer too;
For, bending all my loving thoughts on thee,
The injuries that to myself I do,
Doing thee vantage, double-vantage me.

    Such is my love, to thee I so belong,
    That for thy right myself will bear all wrong.

Reply

These lines come near to being parody
In their admission that the virtue-proof
Of poet's argument—that only he
Had been at fault who'd made his love aloof—

Will be a falsehood. Though the friend's "forsworn,"
A deeper trouble's here in every phrase,
So abject seems the speaker, low, forlorn,
So trampled-tranced in castigating daze.

If he indeed has deemed his friend unfair,
We see him swallow here the beating-stick
That he was hit with. Freedom, though, from care
Is not achieved. 'Twas not a simple trick—

> No, it will be extendedly complex:
> Meek introjection is a wretched hex.

Sonnet 89

Say that thou didst forsake me for some fault,
And I will comment upon that offence:
Speak of my lameness, and I straight will halt,
Against thy reasons making no defence.

Thou canst not, love, disgrace me half so ill,
To set a form upon desired change,
As I'll myself disgrace, knowing thy will.
I will acquaintance strangle, and look strange,

Be absent from thy walks, and in my tongue
Thy sweet beloved name no more shall dwell,
Lest I, too much profane, should do it wrong,
And haply of our old acquaintance tell.

> For thee, against my self I'll vow debate,
> For I must ne'er love him whom thou dost hate.

Reply

To play the role another scripted means
Rejecting personality that's free:
We risk, by acting other-written scenes,
To trample on our actuality.

A ready-made, when stoutly followed through,
Will phantomize and rout essential being.
Whatever's done is mustered for the view
Of stern, pervading "playwright," that in seeing

What he has authored come at length alive,
He may be awed by this, our awful masking,
To be his will-fulfillers when we strive—
Yet deep vacuity confronts our tasking.

    We wish to be applauded, comforted,
    Yet zombie-walk among the living dead.

Sonnet 90

Then hate me when thou wilt, if ever, now,
Now while the world is bent my deeds to cross,
Join with the spite of fortune, make me bow,
And do not drop in for an after-loss:

Ah! do not, when my heart hath 'scap'd this sorrow,
Come in the rearward of a conquer'd woe;
Give not a windy night a rainy morrow
To linger out a purpos'd overthrow.

If thou wilt leave me, do not leave me last
When other petty griefs have done their spite,
But in the onset come: so shall I taste
At first the very worst of fortune's might;

    And other strains of woe, which now seem woe,
    Compar'd with loss of thee, will not seem so.

Reply

A path to speed a healing when you sink
Is knowing there's no remedy for woe:
"The bad take with the bad," and never think
That misery much lower cannot go.

An Irish ditty sings, "The longer you
May live, the sooner you will surely die."
"Let's have the worst right now, on purpose to
Deflate it later" is a futile cry.

"It came to pass" (mind-lifting scripture phrase)
Revival-guidance well may summarize.
"But worse to pass came after," later days
May add, fool-plaint unheard by pluvial skies.

    We'll gravely play a lonely, sighing tune
    Like blinded Odin's, writ in raven-rune.

Sonnet 91

Some glory in their birth, some in their skill,
Some in their wealth, some in their body's force,
Some in their garments though new-fangled ill,
Some in their hawks and hounds, some in their
    horse,

And every humour hath his adjunct pleasure
Wherein it finds a joy above the rest.
But these particulars are not my measure,
All these I better in one gen'ral best.

Thy love is better than high birth to me,
Richer than wealth, prouder than garments' costs,
Of more delight than hawks and horses be;
And having thee, of all men's pride I boast,

    Wretched in this alone, that thou mayst take
    All this away, and me most wretched make.

Reply

The love you mention, meaning everything
To you, can never prove as much to me.
The splendors of a heaven so to sing
As he engenders, those below won't see.

Dantescan hell we dream, as we descend,
With vast variety that life accords.
In paradise the lights that never end
Can not entrance me, though they be the Lord's.

The adjunct pleasures varied humors take,
However, are a lucid eye's delight;
And these, like those, in avid music make
The ravished hearing rival of the sight.

> Phlegmatic, sanguine mood, choleric, sad—
> In shifting hues an ampler heaven's had.

Sonnet 92

But do thy worst to steal thyself away,
For term of life thou art assured mine;
And life no longer than thy love will stay,
For it depends upon that love of thine.

Then need I not to fear the worst of wrongs
When in the least of them my life hath end.
I see a better state to me belongs
Than that which on thy humour doth depend:

Thou canst not vex me with inconstant mind
Since that my life on thy revolt doth lie.
O what a happy title do I find,
Happy to have thy love, happy to die!

    But what's so blessed-fair that fears no blot?
    Thou mayst be false, and yet I know it not.

Reply

Because a human love may altered be
As all things falter underneath the moon,
A Form of Oneness had been dreamed, that we
With higher spheres of Being be in tune.

That nought stay misperceived, belying sight
A deity is made, with flawless eye:
No thing may waver, in that mental might,
In whose wide *esse* we are *percipi*.

Religionists are rare who yet will grant
They cannot care if liked by god or not.
Spinoza was the higher hierophant
Whose own bright love sufficed, the love of thought,

    Unfazed by fading, waning, cataract—
    If yet the agent intellect would act.

Sonnet 93

So shall I live, supposing thou art true,
Like a deceived husband; so love's face
May still seem love to me, though alter'd new;
Thy looks with me, thy heart in other place.

For there can live no hatred in thine eye,
Therefore in that I cannot know thy change.
In many's looks, the false heart's history
Is writ in moods, and frowns, and wrinkles strange.

But heav'n in thy creation did decree
That in thy face sweet love should ever dwell;
Whate'er thy thoughts or thy heart's workings be,
Thy looks should nothing thence but sweetness tell.

    How like Eve's apple doth thy beauty grow
    If thy sweet virtue answer not thy show!

Reply

As, gulled, a husband by a fevered Eve
With wormy apple to the earth was brought,
So here appearance him that would believe
Discomforted in deep-disturbing thought.

For apple palpable may yet appall
If under ruddy-white integument
A canker batten. Then, the angry call
For constancy: "What's this, I beg you? Meant

For venom? Is the charming wisdom tree
For carnal life, or charnel? Fickle flaw!
Our Gen'ral Mother of Inventing, she:
Too wise by half, who laugh at honest law."

    Yet, hallowed-damned by spirit-will to see,
    Their nature isn't faith but inquiry.

Sonnet 94

They that have pow'r to hurt and will do none,
That do not do the thing they most do show,
Who, moving others, are themselves as stone,
Unmoved, cold, and to temptation slow,

They rightly do inherit heaven's graces,
And husband nature's riches from expense;
They are the lords and owners of their faces,
Others but stewards of their excellence.

The summer's flow'r is to the summer sweet
Though to itself it only live and die,
But if that flow'r with base infection meet,
The basest weed outbraves his dignity.

    For sweetest things turn sourest by their deeds:
    Lilies that fester smell far worse than weeds.

Reply

Corruption of the best may be the worst.
They hardest fall who would the highest rise.
Odd supervisors of the world, we first
Have threatened what found favor in our eyes:

Beyond the wildest fright of our surmise
Are oceans climbing, icebergs flow or burst;
With servile pride wherein all splendor dies
We lend ourselves to petty pelf enhearsed

In swollen corporations. Fear denies,
In fungal-mud monopolies immersed,
A spreading temper of accepted lies,
Like acid rain, that have the mind aspersed.

> We can't survive till these be quite reversed.
> Choose life, not death. Be rather blest than curst.

Sonnet 95

How sweet and lovely dost thou make the shame
Which, like a canker in the fragrant rose,
Doth spot the beauty of thy budding name!
O in what sweets dost thou thy sins enclose.

That tongue that tells the story of thy days,
Making lascivious comments on thy sport,
Cannot dispraise, but in a kind of praise,
Naming thy name, blesses an ill report.

O what a mansion have those vices got
Which for their habitation chose out thee,
Where beauty's veil doth cover every blot
And all things turns to fair that eyes can see!

    Take heed, dear heart, of this large privilege:
    The hardest knife ill-us'd doth lose his edge.

Reply

The language, fanciful, may irritate
The casually avid amorist,
And bits of candor can exacerbate
What flattery, insaturate, had kissed.

The path to crisis not a headlong fall
But gradual, declivous, may be made,
And yet, irrévocable, after all,
Can be—when split—to all the world displayed.

If one be husband—the beloved, Eve—
As they were in a former story called,
On sloping road their love will Eden leave
Quite spoiled, if no annoyance be forestalled.

    Our heartened hope the Garden won't fulfill
    Unless by mended friendship tended still.

Sonnet 96

Some say thy fault is youth, some wantonness;
Some say thy grace is youth and gentle sport.
Both grace and faults are lov'd of more and less:
Thou mak'st faults graces that to thee resort.

As on the finger of a throned queen
The basest jewel will be well esteem'd,
So are those errors that in thee are seen
To truths transláted, and for true things deem'd.

How many lambs might the stern wolf betray
If like a lamb he could his looks transláte!
How many gazers mightst thou lead away
If thou wouldst use the strength of all thy state!

    But do not so; I love thee in such sort
    As, thou being mine, mine is thy good report.

Reply

If *traduttore-tradditore* or
Betrayer-by-translation be the gist
Of willed accusal, not the less but more
Might last the languor of the amorist.

"You translate every looseness into beauty,"
So runs the castigating compliment.
But though the scolding's deemed to be a duty,
'Tis clearly, too, as fond caressing lent.

Decoding chiding into flattery,
The speaker shows that he identifies
With all the raptured captivation he
Has known that others in the hero prize.

    So by translation is he, too, betrayed:
    The scapegrace winner, not a sinner, made.

Sonnet 97

How like a winter hath my absence been
From thee, the pleasure of the fleeting year!
What freezings have I felt, what dark days seen!
What old December's bareness everywhere!

And yet this time remov'd was summer's time,
The teeming autumn big with rich increase,
Bearing the wanton burden of the prime
Like widow'd wombs after their lords' decease.

Yet this abundant issue seem'd to me
But hope of orphans and unfather'd fruit;
For summer and his pleasures wait on thee,
And, thou away, the very birds are mute:

> Or, if they sing, 'tis with so dull a cheer
> That leaves look pale, dreading the winter's near.

Reply

To relish the maturing fruitfulness
Of autumn one must view the fertile god—
Adonis, that with food would load and bless
The ground whereon his lovely footsteps trod,

The arms that brought the happy harvest home
Redeeming tearful sowing of the seed,
The golden, holy gleaning from the loam
Where Boaz gave to Ruth what both would need

(Adonis named by Hebrews Adonai).
There is no art without a patron, yet
I don't mean rich maecenas, for what I
And other poets might require will set

> The highest value on a reader who
> Can watch the seed of light, what it will do.

Sonnet 98

From you have I been absent in the spring
When proud-pi'd April, dress'd in all his trim,
Hath put a spirit of youth in everything,
That heavy Saturn laugh'd and leap'd with him.

Yet nor the lays of birds nor the sweet smell
Of different flow'rs in odour and in hue
Could make me any summer's story tell,
Or from their proud lap pluck them where they grew.

Nor did I wonder at the lily's white,
Nor praise the deep vermilion in the rose;
They were but sweet, but figures of delight,
Drawn after you, you pattern of all those.

    Yet seem'd it winter still, and, you away,
    As with your shadow I with these did play.

Reply

To Saturn's happy "reign of sugar candy"—
The old man bent, at last, like Father Time—
Lord Byron dared to raise a toast of brandy
In *Beppo*—entertaining, zany rhyme.

Keats loved the god as much, but saw him sad
And pictured him by tender Thea stroked
Below the eye of Memory, made glad
By empathy, a tragic woe revoked.

As poet, Saturn needs compassion here:
Untimely by a child-god overthrown
(A poet-rival, so we sorely fear),
He in lamenting languishes alone.

> Great Ovid viewed the ancient Age of Gold
> With Saturn glad—old tale retooled, retold.

Sonnet 99

The forward violet thus did I chide:
Sweet thief, whence didst thou steal thy sweet that smells
If not from my love's breath? The purple pride
Which on thy soft cheek for complexion dwells

In my love's veins thou hast too grossly dy'd.
The lily I condemned for thy hand,
And buds of marjoram had stol'n thy hair;
The roses fearfully on thorns did stand,
One blushing shame, another white despair;

A third, nor red nor white, had stol'n of both,
And to his robb'ry had annéx'd thy breath;
But, for his theft, in pride of all his growth
A vengeful canker ate him up to death.

    More flow'rs I noted, yet I none could see
    But sweet or colour it had stol'n from thee.

Reply

When Goethe, in *West-Easterly Divan*,
Desired to laud Zuleika, lady fair,
He made a verbal oriflamme whereon
Islamic attributes of God compare

(All ninety-nine of them, in sacred names)
To those of his beloved worthily.
And justifiably the German claims
That honored so are both the Lord and she.

If here the blossoms want to imitate
Will's godlike friend, then what could be the crime?
To emulate's to praise. In gorgeous state
He ought to celebrate their glory-prime.

> And yet, what rancors crave is rivalry—
> The prideful anger-snake on angel-tree.

Sonnet 100

Where art thou, Muse, that thou forget'st so long
To speak of that which gives thee all thy might?
Spend'st thou thy fury on some worthless song,
Dark'ning thy power to lend base subjects light?

Return, forgetful Muse, and straight redeem
In gentle numbers time so idly spent;
Sing to the ear that doth thy lays esteem
And gives thy pen both skill and argument.

Rise, resty Muse, my love's sweet face survey
If Time have any wrinkle graven there;
If any, be a satire to decay,
And make Time's spoils despised everywhere.

> Give my love fame faster than Time wastes life;
> So thou prevent'st his scythe and crooked knife.

Reply

Not only in Elizabethan days
And in the Renaissance revival-time
Of Italy would fame, with courtly praise,
Make gallivaunting rivals higher climb.

The later Middle Ages blazoned high
Brave Caesar, Hercules, and King René—
Crazed Ajax, Launcelot, and Hector by
Chivalric values bringing into play.

Yet here's no castle hall—on rock of ice
Are names engraven that are melting fast—
King Arthur gone. A writer's kind device
Will honor lauds that William wants to last—

> Appalling sickle held by Father Time
> Dispelled with fine unfickle skill of rhyme.

Sonnet 101

O truant Muse, what shall be thy amends
For thy neglect of truth in beauty dy'd?
Both truth and beauty on my love depends;
So dost thou too, and therein dignifi'd.

Make answer, Muse: wilt thou not haply say,
'Truth needs no colour, with his colour fix'd;
Beauty no pencil, beauty's truth to lay;
But best is best if never intermix'd'?

Because he needs no praise, wilt thou be dumb?
Excuse not silence so, for 't lies in thee
To make him much outlive a gilded tomb
And to be prais'd of ages yet to be.

    Then do thy office, Muse; I teach thee how
    To make him seem long hence as he shows now.

Reply

The love that moved the sun and other stars
In Dante moves the muse and, too, the pen
Of poet here, aid crucial. Silence mars
Unduly merit—his and hers—and then

The reputation of the friend and of
The high inspirer, goddess that the great
Can magnify in growing glory, Love
Won't make more ample. We commiserate

With sad beleaguered poet into whom
She didn't kindly condescend to breathe:
When helped, he'll pencil heav'n in little room,
With fourteen lines entwined a head enwreathe—

    Serene as gleaming-statued classic Greece—
    That "passeth understanding," granting peace.

Sonnet 102

My love is strengthen'd, though more weak in seeming;
I love not less, though less the show appear;
That love is merchandiz'd whose rich esteeming
The owner's tongue doth publish everywhere.

Our love was new and then but in the spring
When I was wont to greet it with my lays
As Philomel in summer's front doth sing
And stops her pipe in growth of riper days:

Not that the summer is less pleasant now
Than when her mournful hymns did hush the night,
But that wild music burthens every bough,
And sweets grown common lose their dear delight.

    Therefore, like her, I sometime hold my tongue
    Because I would not dull you with my song.

Reply

The meek refrain might not reveal esteem
But hide an envy born of rivalry.
Too perfect burden might unlikely seem
As matter for complaint. The hint that he

Set forth in Philomel, who sang but, grieved
And mute, would later brood upon her pain,
Might mean he won't be readily believed
In claiming silence pure perfection's gain.

Yet competition stirs the poet-lyre:
Olympic laurels were awarded for
Proved excellence in flying lyric fire
When forth rhapsodic dithyrambs would pour.

> An agonistic bet means agonies,
> Yet men do better who compete to please.

Sonnet 103

Alack! what poverty my Muse brings forth
That, having such a scope to show her pride,
The argument all bare is of more worth
Than when it hath my added praise beside!

O blame me not if I no more can write!
Look in your glass and there appears a face
That overgoes my blunt invention quite,
Dulling my lines and doing me disgrace.

Were it not sinful then, striving to mend,
To mar the subject that before was well?
For to no other pass my verses tend
Than of your graces and your gifts to tell;

> And more, much more, than in my verse can sit
> Your own glass shows you when you look in it.

Reply

There is a kind of writing which affirms
Ability that, clever, makes from nil,
By contradiction in its major terms,
A testament to unimpeded skill.

The scribe conceives a document to show
That doing so is now impossible—
So Coleridge, in "Dejection," ode of woe;
And Shelley wrote one more, of dolor full,

And Keats penned "Ode on Indolence" to say
That being lazy's too much fun to make
A lyric of, so gladly waved away
Love, Poesy, Ambition. Don't mistake:

> A winningly assumed humility
> Had well assisted William and these three.

Sonnet 104

To me, fair friend, you never can be old,
For as you were when first your eye I ey'd,
Such seems your beauty still. Three winters cold
Have from the forests shook three summers' pride;

Three beauteous springs to yellow autumn turn'd
In process of the seasons have I seen;
Three April pérfumes in three hot Junes burn'd
Since first I saw you fresh, which yet are green.

Ah! yet doth beauty, like a dial hand,
Steal from his figure, and no pace perceiv'd;
So your sweet hue, which methinks still doth stand,
Hath motion, and mine eye may be deceiv'd—

> For fear of which, hear this, thou age unbred:
> Ere you were born was beauty's summer dead.

Reply

If Death is Beauty's mother, as we learn
From Wallace Stevens, then be comforted:
Bold April green, that jealous June will burn,
Is yet—a soul of beauty—never dead.

So Hyacinth and Syrinx, bloom and reed,
In youth florescent, from their tomb arise—
In man and woman, too, at mythic speed
They come again alive, to dry our eyes.

Let dial that sweet Phoebus' race will gauge,
That dew has dampened and the weeping rain,
Declare: what's lovely in each blessed age,
Unlessened, will return—a sun—again.

> Be comforted, and reassure the faint:
> Youths will re-bloom, and Muse their movements
>   paint.

Sonnet 105

Let not my love be call'd idolatry,
Nor my beloved as an idol show,
Since all alike my songs and praises be
To one, of one, still such, and ever so.

Kind is my love today, tomorrow kind,
Still constant in a wondrous excellence;
Therefore my verse to constancy confin'd,
One thing expressing, leaves out difference.

'Fair, kind, and true' is all my argument,
'Fair, kind, and true,' varying to other words;
And in this change is my invention spent,
Three themes in one, which wondrous scope affords.

    Fair, kind, and true have often liv'd alone,
    Which three till now never kept seat in one.

Reply

Then do not count him culpable: no cult
Of polytheic heathen, pagan mage,
Is here, but skiey eidolon, result
Of higher piety defying age

With vision of what humans cannot see,
Assuming each ideal, as Plato said,
To where they'll not become but purely be,
As type and sign whereby our love is led.

He'd not invoke, we note, the Trinity—
It was a time of painting-over saints,
And what had been maintained unchangingly
Was loosed from catechetical constraints—

> But controversy ever swirled above
> All deeper teaching, even Perfect Love.

Sonnet 106

When in the chronicle of wasted time
I see descriptions of the fairest wights,
And beauty making beautiful old rhyme
In praise of ladies dead and lovely knights,

Then, in the blazon of sweet beauty's best,
Of hand, of foot, of lip, of eye, of brow,
I see their ántique pen would have express'd
Ev'n such a beauty as you master now.

So all their praises are but prophecies
Of this our time, all you prefiguring,
And for they looked but with divining eyes,
They had not skill enough your worth to sing:

> For we, which now behold these present days,
> Have eyes to wonder, but lack tongues to praise.

Reply

𝔉our levels Dante sought, that in his text
More meanings, higher-brought, sublime, we'd find.
First literal, and allegoric next,
In old the new predicted, every kind

Of metaphoric exegesis made,
That Jesus we might view in Moses, mind
Alerted that the clues with care were laid,
Fulfilment in foreshadowing divined.

A moral level, too—and then the last,
The anagogic, or the mystical.
The central lesson's Love: we hold it fast.
Past beauties to the friend, prophetic, pull:

> The moral, allegoric, yes. And then—
> Did anagogy also join these men?

Sonnet 107

Not mine own fears nor the prophetic soul
Of the wide world dreaming on things to come
Can yet the lease of my true love control,
Suppos'd as forfeit to a confined doom.

The mortal moon hath her eclipse endur'd,
And the sad augurs mock their own presage;
Incertainties now crown themselves assur'd,
And peace proclaims olives of endless age.

Now with the drops of this most balmy time
My love looks fresh, and Death to me subscribes
Since, spite of him, I'll live in this poor rime
While he insults o'er dull and speechless tribes:

> And thou in this shalt find thy monument
> When tyrants' crests and tombs of brass are spent.

Reply

We learn the symbol: Queen Elizabeth,
Who was the virgin moon, is here bewailed,
Though balmy now, beyond high Dian's death,
Are auspices for James' new-crowning hailed.

And so, the queen is dead, long live the king!
Or, shall we say, the kings? for there are two.
The "regal" minstrel for his friend will sing
In minster of a chamber hid from view.

He'll be the scribe to whom ev'n death subscribes
And, if lamenting yet, be free of fears
And, in admiring, need no tyrant-bribes
But, confident, confront the coming years.

    The one the muses favor, winning, reigns
    With whom the Willing Spirit shares the gains.

Sonnet 108

What's in the brain that ink may character
Which hath not figur'd to thee my true spirit?
What's new to speak, what now to register,
That may express my love or thy dear merit?

Nothing, sweet boy; but yet, like pray'rs divine,
I must each day say o'er the very same,
Counting no old thing old, thou mine, I thine,
Ev'n as when first I hallow'd thy fair name.

So that eternal love in love's fresh case
Weighs not the dust and injury of age
Nor gives to necessary wrinkles place,
But makes antiquity for aye his page,

> Finding the first conceit of love there bred
> Where time and outward form would show it dead.

Reply

Devotions daily may a sameness tempt
In pray'r wheel turning, learning litanies,
In chanting rapid hymn of sense dirempt,
In hallowed listing, whisp'ring rosaries...

Though repetition might enchain the mind,
'Twill viscerally gain sincerity.
Repeated impress on the child, we find,
In depth engraved, avers: 'Yea, verily.'

Repeating is the mother of the feeling
Of truth. When hurled into emergencies,
We view the rueful seekers who are kneeling—
They quail, entreating aid and praying, 'Please!'

> But some are brave: no matter what they've heard,
> They claim that heart and brain begat the word.

Sonnet 109

O never say that I was false of heart,
Though absence seem'd my flame to qualify;
As easy might I from myself depart
As from my soul, which in thy breast doth lie.

That is my home of love: if I have rang'd,
Like him that travels I return again,
Just to the time, not with the time exchang'd,
So that myself bring water for my stain.

Never believe, though in my nature reign'd
All frailties that besiege all kinds of blood,
That it could so prepost'rously be stain'd
To leave for nothing all thy sum of good;

    For nothing this wide universe I call
    Save thou, my rose; in it thou art my all.

Reply

We note again the emblematic rose
That opened all the volume candidly:
It may recall, so commentators gloze,
A fragrant female sexuality.

And we, entranced by Dante's Paradise,
Mark heaven's flow'r: with aromatic balm
The senses' life the spirit will entice
But to enhance the pow'r of wider calm.

The bloom of beauty's charm but sways above
The darker heart of underworldly weal:
To highest patterns of divinest love
Will Pluto-Plutus (buried wealth) appeal.

> The rich-aroma'd rose can so portray
> A rhododactyl-rise from night to day.

Sonnet 110

Alas! 'tis true, I have gone here and there,
And made myself a motley to the view,
Gor'd mine own thoughts, sold cheap what is most dear,
Made old offences of affections new;

Most true it is that I have look'd on truth
Askance and strangely; but, by all above,
These blenches gave my heart another youth,
And worse essáys prov'd thee my best of love.

Now all is done, save what shall have no end:
Mine appetite I never more will grind
On newer proof to try an older friend,
A god in love, to whom I am confin'd.

    Then give me welcome, next my heav'n the best,
    Ev'n to thy pure and most most loving breast.

Reply

What I of repetition wrote before
Will be expanded now in context new
While bringing back a long-forgotten lore—
Yet uncontrollable excitement, too.

Bestirred by deep repentance for what sins
He deemed himself to have committed, he
Who holds fond hope in harness, meek, begins
To make amends, and "most most" lovingly.

So, terrifed by looming, louring cliff,
Had Wordsworth, telling an appalling dream,
The hill called "huge," then "huge" again, as if
He were a cow'ring child. So would it seem

> Our fear, entreaty, protest, eagerness
> Repetitively emphases will press.

Sonnet 111

O for my sake do you with Fortune chide,
The guilty goddess of my harmful deeds,
That did not better for my life provide
Than public means which public manners breeds.

Thence comes it that my name receives a brand,
And almost thence my nature is subdu'd
To what it works in, like the dyer's hand.
Pity me, then, and wish I were renew'd,

Whilst, like a willing patient, I will drink
Potions of eisel 'gainst my strong infection;
No bitterness that I will bitter think,
Nor double penance, to correct correction.

 Pity me then, dear friend, and I assure ye,
 Ev'n that your pity is enough to cure me.

Reply

With all the sympathy I'd like to show
(Not learning what the "harmful" doings were),
I wouldn't chide Fortuna's bounty—no—
For versing is the work Will should prefer—

And that means acting. Hardly an alarm,
Far better gladsome hallelujah he
Might loudly sound for histrionic charm
Of apt chameleon, resplendently

Adorning him with more than dyer's hand
In hues, arrays, and hints of every humor.
I'd counsel, then: reject lamenting and
Heed no dismaying, idle, passing rumor.

    I'm covered in the colors of his mind
    In kindred wise. My fortune's fourteen-lined.

Sonnet 112

Your love and pity doth th' impression fill
Which vulgar scandal stamp'd upon my brow;
For what care I who calls me well or ill,
So you o'er-green my bad, my good allow?

You are my all-the-world, and I must strive
To know my shames and praises from your tongue;
None else to me, nor I to none alive,
That my steel'd sense or changes right or wrong.

In so profound abysm I throw all care
Of others' voices, that my adder's sense
To critic and to flatt'rer stopped are.
Mark how with my neglect I do dispense:

    You are so strongly in my purpose bred
    That all the world besides methinks are dead.

Reply

We find it not unusual for one
Who pioneers in creativity
To need a confidant, when work is done,
As comfort and inspirer, so that he

Can venture forth anew with quickened verve:
Think but of Freud's dependency on Fließ;
And Melville hoped that Hawthorne so might serve;
Ed Ricketts lent John Steinbeck mind-release.

Alone, a poet-nomad wanders far
With "no-man" for a sole identity.
A friend helps lend a feeling that we *are*,
Not merely "evermore about to be."

> Each man's an actor—sadly, this can mean
> A limbo-vision, riddling, in-between.

Sonnet 113

Since I left yóu, mine eye is in my mind,
And that which governs me to go about
Doth part his function and is partly blind,
Seems seeing, but effectually is out;

For it no form delivers to the heart
Of bird, of flow'r, or shape which it doth latch.
Of his quick objects hath the mind no part,
Nor his own vision holds what it doth catch;

For if it see the rud'st or gentlest sight,
The most sweet favour or deformed'st creature,
The mountain or the sea, the day or night,
The crow, or dove, it shapes them to your feature.

    Incapable of more, replete with you,
    My most true mind thus maketh mine untrue.

Reply

We've here a man embarrassed by his riches—
Thus, many-worlded creatures, are we all.
The brain to friend-remembrance quickly switches,
To change the scene and stage. He'll spring—and
    fall!

Preoccupied in scrying an ideal,
We let mundanity be dashed aside:
Colliding, clumsy, with the much-too-real,
We'll in another transient world abide.

Not spatial merely, time-worlds we contain:
Past, present, future. Mythic and historic—
On scale of atom, planet—high, mundane—
The biologic and the allegoric—

    Wide conscious life a wild kaleidoscope,
    Hued, too, with dream-fear, and delight, and
        hope.

Sonnet 114

Or whether doth my mind, being crown'd with you,
Drink up the monarch's plague, this flattery,
Or whether shall I say mine eye saith true,
And that your love taught it this alchemy,

To make of monsters and things indigest
Such cherubins as your sweet self resemble,
Creating every bad a perfect best,
As fast as objects to his beams assemble?

O 'tis the first, 'tis flatt'ry in my seeing,
And my great mind most kingly drinks it up.
Mine eye well knows what with his gust is 'greeing,
And to his palate doth prepare the cup:

>   If it be poison'd, 'tis the lesser sin
>   That mine eye loves it and doth first begin.

Reply

We note a rather complicated way
To state that friendship treats him regally:
But, were it then a curse for him to say
That flatter-words he'll grant veracity,

It nonetheless can be no darksome plot,
This being made to feel that he is brilliant:
What fathers creativity will not
Do harm when built on ego-strength resilient.

Hamletic melancholy—selfish! Go
In gladness, empathetic if quixotic—
Prefer to be deceived in glee than woe.
Be life-love agapetic or erotic,

    The light that is contained within delight
    Blinds less the gaze than pain or vain despite.

Sonnet 115

Those lines that I before have writ do lie,
Ev'n those that said I could not love you dearer;
Yet then my judgment knew no reason why
My most full flame should afterwards burn clearer.

But reck'ning Time, whose million'd accidents
Creep in 'twixt vows, and change decrees of kings,
Tan sacred beauty, blunt the sharp'st intents,
Divert strong minds to th' course of alt'ring things—

Alas! why, fearing of Time's tyranny,
Might I not then say, 'Now I love you best,'
When I was certain o'er incertainty,
Crowning the present, doubting of the rest?

    Love is a babe, then might I not say so,
    To give full growth to that which still doth grow.

Reply

No thing is what it is, for all becomes,
And our becoming's our felicity.
To think about some final bliss benumbs
A mind whose being's dying livingly.

The "solemn troops, and sweet societies
That wipe the tears for ever" from the eyes
In glad Miltonic *Lycidas* can't please
An active man that will require surprise:

The acorn's love is to become an oak
(So Aristotle, *Ethics*), and the tree
Will soon be shedding leaves, new growth to stoke
With mulch—tumultuous, that energy.

> Entelechies crave change for evermore.
> Beyond be borne—else what's a meta phor?

Sonnet 116

Let me not to the marriage of true minds
Admit impediments. Love is not love
Which alters when it alteration finds
Or bends with the remover to remove:

O no, it is an ever-fixed mark,
That looks on tempests and is never shaken;
It is the star to every wand'ring bark,
Whose worth's unknown although his height be
    taken.

Love's not Time's fool, though rosy lips and cheeks
Within his bending sickle's compass come;
Love alters not with his brief hours and weeks,
But bears it out ev'n to the edge of doom.

    If this be error and upon me prov'd,
    I never writ, nor no man ever lov'd.

Reply

I've cited David, Jonathan before
And now again recall their constancy.
So William, too, the rose brought back once more,
Though here as attribute, not essence. He

In cultivating friendship's flower knows
The bloom that in his love he celebrates
May be a Rosicrucian mystic rose
On Eden tree, within the holy gates.

The star that guides the bark of mariners
Had never aught in common with the one
That fell and wrought our ill. Its will demurs
At pride, and must abide till judgement done.

    'Tis love and it alone that justifies
    Our life: the Sun must glow, thus growing wise.

Sonnet 117

𝕬ccuse me thus: that I have scanted all
Wherein I should your great deserts repay,
Forgot upon your dearest love to call
Whereto all bonds do tie me day by day;

That I have frequent been with unknown minds,
And giv'n to time your own dear-purchas'd right;
That I have hoisted sail to all the winds
Which should transport me farthest from your sight.

Book both my wilfulness and errors down,
And on just proof surmise accumulate;
Bring me within the level of your frown,
But shoot not át me in your waken'd hate,

> Since my appeal says I did strive to prove
> The constancy and virtue of your love.

Reply

Adverting to the law and legal terms
Will be a comedy because a crime
Is not in question that attorney-firms
Can fix. Long divagations maritime

To which the wanderer, abashed, alludes
Are nearer to the odyssey of love
Than prosecutors and their petty feuds
The dry-as-dusty lines were talking of.

A parody of passions' pillory:
Alarming charges!—but I simply laughed.
Prefer a trip along a troubled sea,
Abandoned, lacking tackle, on a raft,

> Or dawdling trawler on the foggy main
> To pettifogging lawyers with their train.

Sonnet 118

Like as, to make our appetite more keen,
With eager compounds we our palate urge;
As, to prevent our maladies unseen,
We sicken to shun sickness when we purge;

Ev'n so, being full of your ne'er-cloying sweetness,
To bitter sauces did I frame my feeding,
And, sick of welfare, found a kind of meetness
To be diseas'd, ere that there was true needing.

Thus policy in love, to anticipate
The ills that wére not, grew to faults assur'd
And brought to medicine a healthful state
Which, rank of goodness, would by ill be cur'd,

    But thence I learn and find the lesson true:
    Drugs poison him that so fell sick of you.

Reply

How like an *ars amóris* emblem book
Of images that illustrate the ills
And gifts in friendship, whereupon we look
To learn what anguish or what rapture fills

The alt'ring heart! *Ars amicitiae*—
The famine and the feast of amity.
With wit, the picture-limner wants to play
And fable make in sweet Aesopic glee.

What prophylactic do we learn of here?
What pill designed to purge the surfeited?
Undue suspicion, truly. To endear,
Concern to nervous fear fond love had led.

    Should apprehension stir, averting woe
    We avidly to further worry go.

Sonnet 119

What potions have I drunk of Siren tears
Distill'd from limbecks foul as hell within,
Applying fears to hopes, and hopes to fears,
Still losing when I saw myself to win!

What wretched errors hath my heart committed
Whilst it hath thought itself so blessed never!
How have mine eyes out of their spheres been fitted
In the distraction of this madding fever!

O benefit of ill! now I find true
That better is by evil still made better;
And ruin'd love, when it is built anew,
Grows fairer than at first, more strong, far greater.

    So I return rebuk'd to my content,
    And gain by ill thrice more than I have spent.

Reply

Theodicëans who would justify
(As Milton willed) the ways of God to man,
The good in evil frequently may try
With varied means to find. Some thinkers can

Consider it sufficient to define
The bad as nothing but a lack of good,
To name it no true entity malign,
As if an independent Satan stood,

But just the absence of a better thing.
A clever tactic would be Shakespeare-like:
To prove that evils are essential to
A benefit and boon one loves, a "strike"

    To show a double motive—as a blow
    Or, when we're "striking gold," an end to woe.

Sonnet 120

That you were once unkind befriends me now,
And for that sorrow which I then did feel
Needs must I under my transgression bow
Unless my nerves were brass or hammer'd steel.

For if you were by my unkindness shaken,
As I by yours, you've pass'd a hell of time;
And I, a tyrant, have no leisure taken
To weigh how once I suffer'd in your crime.

O that our night of woe might have remember'd
My deepest sense how hard true sorrow hits,
And soon to you, as you to me, then tender'd
The humble salve which wounded bosoms fits!

    But that your trespass now becomes a fee;
    Mine ransoms yours, and yours must ransom me.

Reply

Salvific is, for amity, the salve
In empathetic, deeply-felt regret.
They merit praise the humbleness who have
Repentance to expand, a signet set

In confirmation of the bonds that last.
For "mutual forgiveness of each vice,"
The love that pardon-virtue had amassed,
Name Paradisal Gate—it will suffice.

Accept your friend, in better and in worst,
Nor ever find in trivial sin a fault,
But framing it in larger picture first,
With gratitude the greater gift exalt.

    Love has the answer. Hail th' unfailing light.
    Take into you totality tonight.

Sonnet 121

'Tis better to be vile than vile esteem'd
When not to be receives reproach of being,
And the just pleasure lost, which is so deem'd
Not by our feeling but by others' seeing:

For why should others' false adult'rate eyes
Give salutation to my sportive blood?
Or on my frailties why are frailer spies,
Which in their wills count bad what I think good?

No, I am that I am, and they that level
At my abuses reckon up their own:
I may be straight though they themselves be bevel;
By their rank thoughts my deeds must not be shown

    Unless this general evil they maintain:
    All men are bad and in their badness reign.

Reply

Though sportive in cavorting, yet he cares
Not much what others will about him say—
For being "what I am" right well declares,
In God-like words, his too's a godly way.

In general, we'd best deflect attention
From what the Other thinks we ought to do.
Creating value makes a brave dimension
To compass—judges competent are few.

Hurray, I say, for one bold mind's denial
Of scrutiny by any but the best.
Let stoners for adul'try stand the trial
Of self-examination—take the test.

> Glass houses prove the proudest virtue frail
> That chained the braver-aimed in irksome jail.

Sonnet 122

Thy gift, thy tables, are within my brain
Full character'd with lasting memory,
Which shall above that idle rank remain,
Beyond all date, ev'n to eternity,

Or, at the least, so long as brain and heart
Have faculty by nature to subsist;
Till each to raz'd oblivion yield his part
Of thee, thy record never can be miss'd.

That poor retention could not so much hold,
Nor need I tallies thy dear love to score;
Therefore to give them fróm me was I bold,
To trust those tables that receive thee more.

    To keep an adjunct to remember thee
    Were to impórt forgetfulness in me.

Reply

No written-down accounts, not even those
Of Thrice Great Hermes that, smarágdine, told
Of higher likened in the low, disclose
The wealth of love, more splendorous than gold.

The abacus can not so tally cash,
Or stick-with-notches trivial victories,
As that which calculation can abash
Will numb'ring mind benumb, defeat with ease—

To wit, the spirit that astounds the letter,
For it's more vast than graven character,
And so can tell of sweet believing better
Than limits of what script you may prefer.

    But that the spirit passeth lettered wit
    I've read, and therefore I remember it.

Sonnet 123

No, Time, thou shalt not boast that I do change:
Thy pyramids built up with newer might
To me are nothing novel, nothing strange;
They are but dressings of a former sight.

Our dates are brief, and therefore we admire
What thou dost foist upon us that is old
And rather make them born to our desire
Than think that we before have heard them told.

Thy registers and thee I both defy,
Not wond'ring at the present nor the past,
For thy recórds and what we see doth lie,
Made more or less by thy continual haste.

    This I do vow and this shall ever be:
    I will be true despite thy scythe and thee.

Reply

Grim reaping scythe, like that by Saturn held—
Old Father Time—which maybe had been used
On him as well, by Jupiter—soon felled
By later doom he'd thought his fate refused—

This cannot make us take a refuge in
The veneration of a pyramid.
Mere length of time the spirit will not win
When death within the building well is hid.

All amplitude pyrámidal is but
The cover of a shrunken mummy-man
Made victim of the reaper's glummer cut
That neither balm nor bandaging will ban.

    If tidal Time require of us a tithe,
    He shan't be master simply with a scythe.

Sonnet 124

𝕴f my dear love were but the child of state,
It might for Fortune's bastard be unfather'd,
As subject to Time's love or to Time's hate,
Weeds among weeds, or flow'rs with flowers gather'd.

No, it was builded far from accident;
It suffers not in smiling pomp nor falls
Under the blow of thralled discontent,
Whereto th' inviting time our fashion calls:

It fears not policy, that heretic,
Which works on leases of short-number'd hours,
But all alone stands hugely politic,
That it nor grows with heat nor drowns with
     showers.

    To this I witness call the fools of Time,
    Which die for goodness, who have lived for crime.

Reply

Disowned or disinherited the friend
Will never be (so here the poet's oath).
The gift of awe, not law, our love won't end—
Thing not factitious, but a soul-seed growth

By smile and crying nourished, sun and rain,
Yet freed from sway of seasons' wayward might,
A yoke not subjugated to that strain
But easy, and the burden of it light—

Not polished by the glib and oily art
That typifies the high affairs of state,
From calculated soilure set apart
Which avid hands to mammon dedicate.

    A deathbed penance, quailingly confessed?
    Grave failure. Never waver from the best.

Sonnet 125

Were't aught to me I bore the canopy,
With my extern the outward honouring,
Or laid great bases for eternity,
Which proves more short than waste or ruining?

Have I not seen dwellers on form and favour
Lose all and more by paying too much rent
For compound sweet forgoing simple savour,
Pitiful thrivers, in their gazing spent?

No, let me be obsequious in thy heart,
And take thou my oblation, poor but free,
Which is not mix'd with seconds, knows no art,
But mutual render, only me for thee.

> Hence, thou suborn'd informer! A true soul
> When most impeach'd stands least in thy
>   control.

Reply

Whereto the tides of timely currents tend,
On that I turned my back, firm traction gaining
In stern resistance to the winning trend,
To lose in favor willing, if retaining

Attraction ampler in fidelity
To muses' love-demand, my hearer-nature.
Tenth hellish circle of self-treachery—
Fixed labels framed by others' nomenclature

With no regard to what we're summoned for—
Will henceforth never hold a place for me.
Rejecting fetters of ungentle lore,
I'll fill my days with Will-to-Poetry,

    No slighter goal embodying my love,
    All smaller, slower light beyond, above.

Sonnet 126

O thou, my lovely boy, who in thy power
Dost hold Time's fickle glass, his fickle hour;
Who hast by waning grown, and therein show'st
Thy lovers with'ring, as thy sweet self grow'st,

If Nature, sov'reign mistress over wrack,
As thou go'st onwards, still will pluck thee back,
She keeps thee to this purpose: that her skill
May time disgrace and wretched minutes kill.

Yet fear her, O thou minion of her pleasure!
She may detain, but not still keep, her treasure:

> Her audit (though delay'd) answer'd must be,
> And her quiétus is to render thee.

Reply

By scythe and by the hourglass threatened, why
Had then the friend's attraction lately grown?
Maturing, ripening, he'll gratify,
Assuring fair complexion doubly shown,

But now the threat is likewise doubled, for
Old Time, who hates to find his power mocked,
Will soon foreclose the mortage, all the more
Intent on claiming debt by contract clocked.

So—Nature versus Time—is rivalry
The reason why the good die often young?
And is the wooing fired by jealousy
Or moved by mooted right in pride, high-strung?

    The twelve-line lyric a diminished will
    Portrays, brief réspite, maybe, left, until—

Sonnet 127

In the old age black was not counted fair,
Or if it were, it bore not beauty's name;
But now is black beauty's successive heir,
And beauty slander'd with a bastard shame:

For since each hand hath put on Nature's power,
Fairing the foul with Art's false borrow'd face,
Sweet beauty hath no name, no holy bower,
But is profan'd, if not lives in disgrace.

Therefore my mistress' eyes are raven black,
Her eyes so suited, and they mourners seem
At such who, not born fair, no beauty lack,
Sland'ring creation with a false esteem:

> Yet so they mourn, becoming of their woe,
> That every tongue says beauty should look so.

Reply

With all the twisting, restlessly complex,
With all the wit that well may lead amiss
And, thick in syntax, twinned in meaning, vex,
A fitting theme is treated—namely, this:

That darker skin, brows, eyes, and hair undyed
Are far more favored than they used to be,
So, now, the lady's features, glorified
In later days, we may more truly see.

Though Solomon a beauty black would laud,
Yet some maintained the fine must be the "fair."
Abetted by cosmetics they'd applaud,
Proud counterfeits would every day prepare.

    Yet when in anthems "lady fair" I find,
    "I'm black and comely" rather comes to mind.

Sonnet 128

How oft when thou, my music, music play'st,
Upon that blessed wood whose motion sounds
With thy sweet fingers when thou gently sway'st
The wiry concord that mine ear confounds,

Do I envý those jacks that nimble leap,
To kiss the tender inward of thy hand,
Whilst my poor lips which should that harvest reap,
At the wood's boldness by thee blushing stand!

To be so tickled, they would change their state
And situation with those dancing chips
O'er whom thy fingers walk with gentle gait,
Making dead wood more bless'd than living lips.

    Since saucy jacks so happy are in this,
    Give them thy fingers, me thy lips to kiss.

Reply

She is a music in herself, who plays
While touching eager jacks (or keys, or men)
Upon the virginal in pleasing ways,
Intact—untouched by lips—indeed, but then

Im Takt (the German phrase that means in pace
Or time or rhythm), and upon the heart,
She'll, eager, fond of harvest gleaning, race
And take, in leap of gleaming keys, a part.

Too far apart, alas! are they from Will—
Yet might the player nearly be a Muse,
Tune choiring in his mind as well, to fill,
Apollo-bright, love-lyring lines, infuse

    A happy handsomeness into the dance
    That had re-manned him with a gladsome
        trance.

Sonnet 129

Th' expense of spirit in a waste of shame
Is lust in action: and till action, lust
Is perjur'd, murd'rous, bloody, full of blame,
Savage, extreme, rude, cruel, not to trust;

Enjoy'd no sooner but despised straight,
Past reason hunted, and no sooner had
Past reason hated, as a swallow'd bait
On purpose laid to make the taker mad:

Mad in pursuit and in possession so;
Had, having, and in quest to have, extreme;
A bliss in proof, and prov'd, a very woe;
Before, a joy propos'd; behind, a dream.

> All this the world well knows; yet none knows well
> To shun the heav'n that leads men to this hell.

Reply

"But what is lust if not desire and want?
Inseparable therefore, too, from Will?"
Grave Schopenhauer taught: "The love we vaunt
In fiery drive is blind, unstopping still,

Unseeing that there may abide no rest
Unless all want be stifled, blood and blame
Be shunned along with pleasures deemed the best:
Pain, pleasure are alike, one Will their name.

Another name for Will is fiery Wheel—
To whirl and hurl. So—time to call a halt.
Desire no disillusioning Ideal!
From world be turned away, for want's a fault."

    Yet, Prospero, don't toss that lusty book!
    Desire, as Life, let shine in lover's look.

Sonnet 130

My mistress' eyes are nothing like the sun;
Coral is far more red than her lips' red:
If snow be white, why then her breasts are dun;
If hairs be wires, black wires grow on her head.

I have seen roses damask'd, red and white,
But no such roses see I in her cheeks;
And in some pérfumes is there more delight
Than in the breath that from my mistress reeks.

I love to hear her speak, yet well I know
That music hath a far more pleasing sound:
I grant I never saw a goddess go;
My mistress, when she walks, treads on the ground.

    And yet, by heav'n, I think my love as rare,
    As any she belied with false compare.

Reply

𝔍f maidens are belied with likeness fake
They'll gain from tactics advocated here.
Their reputation candor cannot shake:
Portrayals accurate are beauty's peer.

With clearer view you needn't fear to lose
The cheer of charm that compliments commend.
Since honesty no merit will refuse
Depicting, there is nought a fib will lend.

Yet, false comparisons all tossed away,
We'd best not jettison, as well, the true.
A sunny eye, a singing laugh, I say,
Convey a gentle maid in lover's view.

    And what of smiling light, or speaking eye?
    If novelty elate, I rate them high.

Sonnet 131

Thou art as tyrannous, so as thou art,
As those whose beauties proudly make them cruel;
For well thou know'st to my dear doting heart
Thou art the fairest and most precious jewel.

Yet, in good faith, some say that thee behold,
Thy face hath not the pow'r to make love groan.
To say they err I dare not be so bold,
Although I swear it to myself alone;

And to be sure that is not false I swear,
A thousand groans, but thinking on thy face,
One on another's neck, do witness bear
Thy black is fairest in my judgment's place.

> In nothing art thou black save in thy deeds,
> And thence this slander, as I think, proceeds.

Reply

Her beauty multiplied a thousandfold—
If we may gauge it by the numbered groans—
In dark and splendid ray of solar gold,
She's yet subjected to unpleasant tones.

We mark the metaphor of black for bad
As in the murky verb "to denigrate,"
Which I deplore, would rather not have had
In lingual legacy—it led to hate

And hexed, in sadder chapter, histories.
Yet "black is fairest"—*that* I like to read!
And should an action happen to displease,
And worthy of reproof be deemed, then heed:

>It's twice unfair that "fair" be doubly so,
>And black-as-bad one likewise would forgo.

Sonnet 132

Thine eyes I love, and they, as pitying me,
Knowing thy heart tormént me with disdain,
Have put on black and loving mourners be,
Looking with pretty ruth upon my pain.

And truly not the morning sun of heaven
Better becomes the grey cheeks of the east,
Nor that full star that ushers in the even
Doth half that glory to the sober west,

As those two mourning eyes become thy face:
O let it then as well beseem thy heart
To mourn for me since mourning doth thee grace
And suit thy pity like in every part.

> Then will I swear beauty herself is black,
> And all they foul that thy complexion lack.

Reply

Dark eve-and-morning Venus—light in black—
Are rays of raven eyes that make him rave.
Ruth, pitying, is pretty, too, in lack
Made sad, yet in compassion quick to save.

The lovely star that ushered in our eve
Will herald ever-rosy dawn as well.
They're both the selfsame lumen, so believe
What soothed in sleep fine wakeful tale will tell.

Sweet Hesper-Phosphor oft had comfort lent
By thoughts of destined rising from the night
And echoed from the vasty firmament
The lasting vesper-matin of the light.

    So wishes can be granted, eyes be filled
    With brightness in the sighing night distilled.

Sonnet 133

Beshrew that heart that makes my heart to groan
For that deep wound it gives my friend and me!
Is't not enough to torture me alone,
But slave to slavery my sweet'st friend must be?

Me from myself thy cruel eye hath taken,
And my next self thou harder hast engross'd:
Of him, myself, and thee I am forsaken,
A torment thrice threefóld thus to be cross'd.

Prison my heart in thy steel bosom's ward,
But then my friend's heart let my poor heart bail;
Whoe'er keeps me, let mý heart be his guard;
Thou canst not then use rigour in my jail.

    And yet thou wilt; for I, being pent in thee,
    Perforce am thine, and all that ís in me.

Reply

The keeper, she, behold! of threefold prison—
With friend and William, they the triple warden.
From lovers' hell no souls have, rescued, risen:
All hope abandon, entered here—no pardon.

And yet the guards are each a prisoner—
They bear love's manacles and mental burden,
Refrain discordant, for they don't concur,
Sad-happy care their fetter and their guerdon.

Convicted, if with scant conviction—three
Co-sufferers in dungeon-passion pent—
They won't escape since, cleft internally,
Affection binds what rivalry has rent.

    We may suppose the lady hopes her friends'
    Unspent affection, threatened, never ends.

Sonnet 134

So, now I have confess'd that he is thine,
And I myself am mortgag'd to thy will,
Myself I'll forfeit, so that other mine
Thou wilt restore to be my comfort still:

But thou wilt not, nor he will not be free,
For thou art covetous, and he is kind;
He learn'd but surety-like to write for me
Under that bond that him as fast doth bind.

The statute of thy beauty thou wilt take,
Thou usurer, that put'st forth all to use,
And sue a friend came debtor for my sake;
So him I lose through my unkind abuse.

> Him have I lost; thou hast both him and me:
> He pays the whole, and yet am I not free.

Reply

She's called Priscilla Mullins, and poor Will
Miles Standish, and John Alden is the friend.
Two roommates' amity is grand until
A messenger is Alden made, to lend

Some polish to his comrade's keen proposal.
Priscilla isn't backward, straightaway
(Though she respects the errand-boy, no losel)
Must hint she'd like to see him more some day.

Will's friend, like Alden, seems the guarantor
And representative and emissary.
Had Will but known whom he'd be working for
Too soon, he'd likelier have been more wary.

    Inferno Henry Wadsworth rendered well;
    Of *Sonnets*, too, he worthy news would tell.

Sonnet 135

Whoever hath her wish, thou hast thy 'Will,'
And 'Will' to boot, and 'Will' in overplus;
More than enough am I that vex'd thee still,
To thy sweet will making addition thus.

Wilt thou, whose will is large and spacïous,
Not once vouchsafe to hide my will in thine?
Shall will in others seem right gracïous
And in my will no fair acceptance shine?

The sea, all water, yet receives rain still
And in abundance addeth to his store;
So thou, being rich in 'Will,' add to thy 'Will'
One will of mine, to make thy large will more.

    Let no unkind 'No' fair beseechers kill;
    Think all but one, and me in that one 'Will.'

Reply

The World as Will—to gloze that notion I
Spoke, not too long ago, of Schopenhauer.
The great "I am" becomes "I will," for why
Be shy of crying that desire is power?

The Grand Unconscious, Blind Imagination,
It scatters with unfathomed amplitude
What Maker-venerators call creation,
But emanation's better. Cruel, crude,

Relentless in the driving of Desire,
It spawns, at times, a true poetic seër.
With calm detachment, stilling will-stoked fire,
He'll deeply view the world as pure Idea.

    Art, distancing, controlling, reinvents
    The Will, to bend it to its own intents.

Sonnet 136

If thy soul check thee that I come so near,
Swear to thy blind soul that I was thy 'Will,'
And will, thy soul knows, is admitted there;
Thus far for love, my love-suit, sweet, fulfil.

'Will' will fulfil the treasure of thy love,
Ay, fill it full with wills, and my will one.
In things of great receipt with ease we prove
Among a number one is reckon'd none.

Then in the number let me pass untold,
Though in thy store's account I one must be;
For nothing hold me, so it please thee hold
That nothing me, a something sweet to thee:

> Make but my name thy love, and love that still,
> And then thou lov'st me for my name is 'Will.'

Reply

Let these two wills be one, that one be Will.
Then will he always have his will: you see?
United namely, they might coo and bill,
For Bill is Will and willing, also she—

For thought and rhyme and homonym agree
In wanton ways that William's mind may thrill
And rivalries that riled him recently
With euphony bemusedly can still.

So wiser wit will sly suspicion kill:
Let guile and guilt and crafty planning be
By imbibition from a Lethe-rill
Of magic language, William-wizardry,

    Undone. A lulling, pacifying pill
    Can with an awesome calmness grant good will.

Sonnet 137

Thou blind fool, Love, what dost thou to mine eyes,
That they behold, and see not what they see?
They know what beauty is, see where it lies,
Yet what the best is take the worst to be.

If eyes, corrupt by over-partial looks,
Be anchor'd in the bay where all men ride,
Why of eyes' falsehood hast thou forged hooks
Whereto the judgement of my heart is tied?

Why should my heart think that a several plot
Which my heart knows the wide world's common
      place?
Or mine eyes, seeing this, say this is not,
To put fair truth upon so foul a face?

    In things right true my heart and eyes have err'd,
    And to this false plague are they now transferr'd.

Reply

Unseaworthy for love, this boat that's been—
In harbor, even—plundered and dismasted—
Too welcoming by far, the bard had seen,
Who, long deprived of heart-supply, had fasted.

For if the mythic siren came to shore,
Waylaying there the sailors in their haven,
Her call should warn the mariner the more
Before her grasping lines on heart were graven.

Adventure beckons in the tempting bay
But must by ev'ry tactic be resisted
Lest thought in some unprofitable fray
To serve a crass commander be enlisted.

> A Helen-figurehead upon a prow
> To ill has led, is leading. Leave it now.

Sonnet 138

When my love swears that she is made of truth,
I do believe her though I know she lies,
That she might think me some untutor'd youth
Unlearned in the world's false subtleties.

Thus vainly thinking that she thinks me young,
Although she knows my days are past the best,
Simply I credit her false-speaking tongue:
On both sides thus is simple truth suppress'd.

But wherefore says she not she is unjust?
And wherefore say not I that I am old?
O love's best habit is in seeming trust,
And age, in love, loves not to have years told:

    Therefore I lie with her, and she with me,
    And in our faults by lies we flatter'd be.

Reply

She seems unfaithful, he appears unyoung—
About their weaknesses they like to lie.
I have to say that, were this love unsung,
The world would be depleted, as would I.

Let fiction then continue, let it thrive:
Illusion, loving ever were entwined—
The pink-hued glasses gladness can revive,
Repelling enmity, delights to find.

Sheherazade made dramas every day
And then declaimed them to the king at night;
Thus artistry had found a winning way
Of soundly counterfeiting heart's delight.

    Then if you cannot love me, love my lies:
    They'll be for us the fairer paradise.

Sonnet 139

O call not me to justify the wrong
That thy unkindness lays upon my heart;
Wound me not with thine eye, but with thy tongue:
Use pow'r with pow'r, and slay me not by art.

Tell me thou lov'st elsewhere; but in my sight,
Dear heart, forbear to glance thine eye aside:
What need'st thou wound with cunning, when thy might
Is more than my o'erpress'd defence can bide?

Let me excuse thee: ah! my love well knows
Her pretty looks have been mine enemies;
And therefore from my face she turns my foes,
That they elsewhere might dart their injuries.

   Yet do not so; but since I am near slain,
   Kill me outright with looks, and rid my pain.

Reply

I'm touched by this—the vulnerable way
He'd like to save a shaky situation.
Though risky, simple would it be to say,
"Her glances are a blatant provocation

And for that reason promptly should be stopped."
For she is pretty—there is competition...
The problem isn't one that can be dropped—
A far more complicated proposition.

When Pushkin, greatest Russian poet, married
A lovely maiden praised and celebrated,
He learned her would-be lovers dallied, tarried,
And, deeming happiness adulterated,

>He fumed with envy, an exploding fuel,
>And, pistol loading, perished in a duel.

Sonnet 140

Be wise as thou art cruel; do not press
My tongue-tied patience with too much disdain,
Lest sorrow lend me words, and words express
The manner of my pity-wanting pain.

If I might teach thee wit, better it were,
Though not to love, yet, love, to tell me so,
As testy sick men, when their deaths be near,
No news but health from their physicians know;

For, if I should despair, I should grow mad
And in my madness might speak ill of thee:
Now this ill-wresting world is grown so bad,
Mad sland'rers by mad ears believed be.

> That I may not be so, nor thou beli'd,
> Bear thine eyes straight, though thy proud heart go wide.

Reply

He's asking her for pacifying lies,
With ev'n her narrowed glance a blank untruth.
But self-respect, so mortified, will rise
In tender penitence, remorse, and ruth.

If he'd prefer a fiction, then he'd best
Be counseled rather to create his own—
Her daring dereliction lends no rest
And won't be righted by reproaches thrown.

Deception will engender more deceit.
She can't be your dramatic character...
Command in letters, with intention sweet,
Invention independently of her!

    Eyes travel? So the soul may wander far:
    They cavil not who have a polar star.

Sonnet 141

In faith I do not love thee with mine eyes,
For they in thee a thousand errors note;
But 'tis my heart that loves what they despise,
Who, in despite of view, is pleased to dote.

Nor are mine ears with thy tongue's tune delighted,
Nor tender feeling, to base touches prone,
Nor taste, nor smell, desire to be invited
To any sensual feast with thee alone:

But my five wits nor my five senses can
Dissuade one foolish heart from serving thee,
Who leaves unsway'd the likeness of a man,
Thy proud heart's slave and vassal wretch to be.

    Only my plague thus far I count my gain,
    That she that makes me sin awards me pain.

Reply

What funny comedown from her former glory:
Postmortal woe by pain abated here!
The stay will shortened be in Purgatory,
With lessened torment—splendid form of cheer.

Unblamed is the beloved lady; she
Has far too many failings to be chidden.
The singer seems delirious, for he
Does willingly, in prison, what he's bidden.

Will earlier had asked his friend to have
Ten children fair, to spread his likeness wide.
Now tenfold sense and wit, no saving salve,
Are bowed and bent and broken. There abide

>Alone the present plague, the gain postponed
>Till after pain outgrown and plaint outgroaned.

Sonnet 142

Love is my sin, and thy dear virtue hate,
Hate of my sin, grounded on sinful loving:
O but with mine compare thou thine own state,
And thou shalt find it merits not reproving;

Or, if it do, not from those lips of thine,
That have profan'd their scarlet ornaments
And seal'd false bonds of love as oft as mine,
Robb'd others' beds' revénues of their rents.

Be it lawful I love thee, as thou lov'st those
Whom thine eyes woo as mine impórtune thee:
Root pity in thy heart, that, when it grows,
Thy pity may deserve to piti'd be.

> If thou dost seek to have what thou dost hide,
> By self-example mayst thou be deni'd!

Reply

It is a pitiable exhibition—
And pitiless, reciprocal disclosure.
Red-tinted lips have robbed: in this perdition
The poet mirrored lent a self-exposure.

The scarlet ornament and carmine seal
Have little of the whiteness of the snow—
Incarnadine, garb ardent will reveal
The virtues cardinal gone long ago.

And candor banishment commands to be
Not polished, planished, but acknowledged true;
As pitiful as guilt, admittedly,
Yet pity well may bring forgiveness, too.

> With accusation lessened in confession
> A rancor-dampener's the venting session.

Sonnet 143

𝕷o, as a careful housewife runs to catch
One of her feather'd creatures broke away,
Sets down her babe, and makes all swift dispatch
In pùrsuit of the thing she would have stay,

Whilst her neglected child holds her in chase,
Cries to catch hér whose busy care is bent
To follow that which flies before her face,
Not prizing her poor infant's discontent;

So runn'st thou after that which flies from thee
Whilst I thy babe chase thee afar behind,
But if thou catch thy hope, turn back to me,
And play the mother's part, kiss me, be kind;

    So will I pray that thou mayst have thy 'Will'
    If thou turn back and my loud crying still.

Reply

A Freudian would levitate, for here
(Portrayed with entertaining levity)
Our Will's annoyed and wants a mother near:
She rounds up fowls; he's howling, "Look at me!"

As verb the "still" means he'll be quieted
The moment she relaxes and returns.
But read as adverb, "still" means: even fed
With full attention, "yet" the infant yearns

And cries and can't be rightly satisfied.
A drive insatiable, the baby's will!
The need for nourishment, too long denied,
Not quite can ever surrogate fulfill.

    If child on parent pattern all desire,
    To after-image cries will rise yet higher.

Sonnet 144

Two loves I have, of comfort and despair,
Which like two spirits do suggest me still:
The better angel is a man right fair,
The worser spirit a woman colour'd ill.

To win me soon to hell, my female evil
Tempteth my better angel from my side
And would corrupt my saint to be a devil,
Wooing his purity with her foul pride.

And whether that my angel be turn'd fiend,
Suspect I may, yet not directly tell;
But being both from me, both to each friend,
I guess one angel in another's hell:

> Yet this shall I ne'er know, but live in doubt,
> Till my bad angel fire my good one out.

Reply

Inaugurating reconciliation,
Convoking an enlightened legislature,
Abe Lincoln, speaking deeply to the nation,
Had hoped "the better angels of our nature"

Would "touch the mystic chords of memory"
And move the harp and heart to brotherhood:
In such an import-holding image he
Evoked a love-hope as no other could.

The "better angel" and the "worser spirit"
Have waged in Will unlovely civil war:
A scripture-tinged psychómachy (we hear it)
Contrásts, alas, with Lincoln's hallowed lore.

    Bewildered, will-divided manichee,
    Good, ill—that vie within—he cannot flee.

Sonnet 145

Those lips that Love's own hand did make
Breathed forth the sound that said 'I hate'
To me that languish'd for her sake:
But when she saw my woeful state,

Straight in her heart did mercy come,
Chiding that tongue that ever sweet
Was us'd in giving gentle doom,
And taught it thus anew to greet:

'I hate' she alter'd with an end
That followed it as gentle day
Doth follow night, who like a fiend
From heav'n to hell is flown away.

    'I hate' from hate away she threw,
    And sav'd my life, saying 'not you.'

Reply

How sprightly and how swift and how
Delightful—spirit-lifting, she:
Compassionating lady—row
And louring done—recovery!

The four-beat scheme portrayed the speed
(One fifth increased, in brief) whereby
A word became a healing deed
Wherein a seed of light would lie.

A sunray, rapid, quickening,
A dozen lines, and comfort's had.
I hear the gentle lady sing,
"I hate, just hate—to make you sad."

Sonnet 146

Poor soul, the centre of my sinful earth,
[   ] these rebel powers array,
Why dost thou pine within and suffer dearth,
Painting thy outward walls so costly gay?

Why so large cost, having so short a lease,
Dost thou upon thy fading mansion spend?
Shall worms, inheritors of this excess,
Eat up thy charge? Is this thy body's end?

Then soul, live thou upon thy servant's loss,
And let that pine to aggravate thy store.
Buy terms divine in selling hours of dross;
Within be fed, without be rich no more:

> So shalt thou feed on Death, that feeds on men,
> And Death once dead, there's no more dying then.

Reply

Beyond the "first death," Dylan Thomas wrote,
"There is no other," as he meditated
On Bible and on Shakespeare, likely. Note
Advancing ravage, haply intimated

By fabric-hole, a symbol. Ills and moths,
Like rust, corrupt, and leave the body gone,
Which is the longest-lived of spirit-cloths,
A garment set aside. An ardent swan,

Soul rising, white as parchment, leaves behind
The lasting testament of canorous
And candid palest page, which us that find
Enlivens with an anthem amorous.

    Live therefore ever in my heart and mind,
    Enkindling sun, encompassing and kind.

Sonnet 147

𝔐y love is as a fever longing still
For that which longer nurseth the disease,
Feeding on that which doth preserve the ill,
Th' uncertain sickly appetite to please.

My reason, the physician to my love,
Angry that his prescriptions are not kept,
Hath left me, and I desp'rate now approve
Desire is death, which physic did except.

Past cure I am, now Reason is past care,
And frantic-mad with evermore unrest:
My thoughts and my discourse as madmen's are,
At random from the truth vainly express'd;

> For I have sworn thee fair, and thought thee bright,
> Who art as black as hell, as dark as night.

Reply

So Death and Maiden, compassed in Desire,
That with high flow and disabusing ebb
Is paradigm of that bipolar fire
Which those entrapped in life-death spiderweb

May feel as heaven-hell—my repertory
Of metaphoric emblems crazy-ranges
Among the elements, a madding story
Of horrible unmotivated changes.

Say "love" and "vulnerable"—they are one:
And therefore doctor and disease are blended.
With symptoms are we never wholly done—
When shaken once, all surety is ended.

> Yet harm not mercy-cured is purged in art,
> The physic, perfect, of the hurt in heart.

Sonnet 148

O me! what eyes hath Love put in my head,
Which have no correspondence with true sight;
Or, if they have, where is my judgement fled,
That censures falsely what they see aright?

If that be fair whereon my false eyes dote,
What means the world to say it is not so?
If it be not, then love doth well denote
Love's eye is not so true as all men's: no,

How can it, O how can Love's eye be true,
That is so vex'd with watching and with tears?
No marvel, then, though I mistake my view;
The sun itself sees not till heaven clears.

    O cunning Love! with tears thou keep'st me blind,
    Lest eyes well-seeing thy foul faults should find.

Reply

More sweet the tone in all the melody
That's made (line nine) by loved and sudden "O"
In ample assonantal harmony
With "no" (line eight) and (in line ten) with "so."

The deathlier, more hellish, the lament
The more the music proved the man alive.
By this to melancholy languor's lent
A charm. Tchaikovsky, in his number five,

The manic-tragic, lent that double gift—
Uplifting symphony, through huger gloom.
So love and object, if unbridged the rift,
Are linked theurgic antidote to doom.

    The sonnet cycle, by melodic skill,
    With eye-dew says "I do," weds good with ill.

Sonnet 149

Canst thou, O cruel, say I love thee not
When I against myself with thee partake?
Do I not think on thee when I forgot
Am of my self, all tyrant, for thy sake?

Who hateth thee that I do call my friend?
On whom frown'st thou that I do fawn upon?
Nay, if thou lour'st on me, do I not spend
Revenge upon myself with present moan?

What merit do I in my self respect,
That is so proud thy service to despise,
When all my best doth worship thy defect,
Commanded by the motion of thine eyes?

    But, love, hate on, for now I know thy mind;
    Those that can see thou lov'st, and I am blind.

Reply

When vexed by love, he knows he overfrets—
And this will irritate the lady. He
Knows *that*, as well, and so he plainly sets
The matter in perspective: blindingly,

Neuroses lower him that feels the woe,
And yet when recognized will elevate
His blurry tears envisioned clearly—so
Dispel what error-fret may flow in spate.

Not easy, inner strife like this to bear,
When worst and best, combining, blend in burst:
And yet accepting melded foul and fair
Will free resentment-strength when deep enhearsed.

    Free utterance, deep love, when partnering,
    Can charm the will, and thus can wisdom sing.

Sonnet 150

O from what pow'r hast thou this pow'rful might
With insufficiency my heart to sway,
To make me give the lie to my true sight
And swear that brightness doth not grace the day?

Whence hast thou this becoming of things ill,
That in the very refuse of thy deeds
There is such strength and warrantise of skill
That, in my mind, thy worst all best exceeds?

Who taught thee how to make me love thee more,
The more I hear and see just cause of hate?
O though I love what others do abhor,
With others thou shouldst not abhor my state:

> If thy unworthiness rais'd love in me,
> More worthy I to be belov'd of thee.

Reply

He says, "You make me love you, and you're bad;
Your badness makes me love you, so you ought,
If I'm made bad by love, to love me—sad
From others' standpoint, but at least the thought

Of badness in your Will can not dissuade
Your own bad love from being active for
The bad one who is loving you the more,
The more he feels by you his badness made."

I know the reader finds it all quite clear
Now I have simplified the train of mind
And, charmed to play the role of teacher here,
Have chalked a blackboard full, words underlined.

> That is our clever lesson for today—
> So please don't wipe those helpful lines away.

Sonnet 151

Love is too young to know what conscience is,
Yet who knows not conscience is born of love?
Then, gentle cheater, urge not my amiss,
Lest guilty of my faults thy sweet self prove:

For, thou betraying me, I do betray
My nobler part to my gross body's treason;
My soul doth tell my body that he may
Triumph in love; flesh stays no farther reason,

But rising at thy name doth point out thee
As his triumphant prize. Proud of this pride,
He is contented thy poor drudge to be,
To stand in thy affairs, fall by thy side.

    No want of conscience hold it that I call
    Her 'love,' for whose dear love I rise and fall.

Reply

I had a battle-standard rising high
Before I could identify whose gift—
Disarming all who might the same espy!—
Made *Fascinans* a happy hope to lift.

What magic staff that, dome-formed oriflamme
Of Cupid bearing, independent, stands—
Except of him who, docile as a lamb
In cute appearance, utters mute commands.

If Augustine, unawed and angered by
A body organ so impolitic,
Had called its rise a fall from Eden high
To ill, despondent swamp, an impish trick,

> I call its fall a fall, its rise a rise:
> Long may its grace find favor in our eyes!

Sonnet 152

In loving thee thou know'st I am forsworn,
But thou art twice forsworn, to me love swearing;
In act thy bed-vow broke, and new faith torn
In vowing new hate after new love bearing.

But why of two oaths' breach do I accuse thee
When I break twenty? I am perjur'd most;
For all my vows are oaths but to misuse thee,
And all my honest faith in thee is lost.

For I have sworn deep oaths of thy deep kindness,
Oaths of thy love, thy truth, thy constancy,
And, to enlighten thee, gave eyes to blindness,
Or made them swear against the thing they see;

> For I have sworn thee fair: more perjur'd eye,
> To swear against the truth so foul a lie!

Reply

If truly we've not dropped the Cupid theme—
And I'm enamored of it, in my manner—
Abounding vows will yet as futile seem
As wishing sprindrift to the rapid-scanner.

He swore that she was fair—this can't imply
That she will never deal with him unfairly.
Should he, more witting, hear a witty lie,
He will not witness falsely, but awarely.

Yet Cupid may the brain quite witless make:
He is cupidity, and that is greedy.
Avidity in him is no mistake,
For it is nature that has made him needy.

    Then all for love! Or nothing—either way,
    Obrumpent bubble-game, compulsive play.

Sonnet 153

Cupid laid by his brand and fell asleep:
A maid of Dian's this advantage found
And his love-kindling fire did quickly steep
In a cold valley-fountain of that ground,

Which borrow'd from this holy fire of Love
A dateless lively heat, still to endure,
And grew a seething bath, which yet men prove
Against strange maladies a sov'reign cure.

But at my mistress' eye Love's brand new-fired,
The boy for trial needs would touch my breast;
I, sick withal, the help of bath desired
And thither hied, a sad distemper'd guest,

> But found no cure, the bath for my help lies
> Where Cupid got new fire, my mistress' eyes.

Reply

I'd go a-dowsing, Will, if I were you—
With simple stick of golden bough divine
To bring a newer geyser into view,
Or hidden Hippocrene more Ápolline.

The one will warm, the other cool you down,
Though latterly the latter, too, may heat—
Poetic furor, if no Fury-frown,
May madden, oracle be bitter-sweet.

Both Cupid and Apollo oft have brought
A plaguy, labile weather of the soul
That drove the steed of love to frustrate thought
(With Phoebus, Hyacinth). But, on the whole,

> You're prudent, courting laureled Poetry,
> Pursuing lesser peril, verily.

Sonnet 154

The little Love-god lying once asleep
Laid by his side his heart-inflaming brand,
Whilst many nymphs that vow'd chaste life to keep
Came tripping by; but in her maiden hand

The fairest votary took up that fire
Which many legions of true hearts had warm'd:
And so the general of hot desire
Was, sleeping, by a virgin hand disarm'd.

This brand she quenched in a cool well by,
Which from Love's fire took heat perpetual,
Growing a bath and healthful remedy,
For men diseas'd; but I, my mistress' thrall,

    Came there for cure and this by that I prove:
    Love's fire heats water, water cools not love.

Reply

Love-hymns are mind-flame and will duly last,
Convey their lordly, meta-phoric, fond
Enkindling, while, by spirit-lore made fast,
They, root-wise, truly, "carry" us "beyond."

Love lyrics can transmit a twofold treasure
By making blood run swiftly through the frame
As, ardently in carmine heartbeat measure,
They intimate the heav'ns no man might name.

Eyes, bright, are dampened while I'm writing this!
I say it unabashed and reft of shame—
A dithyramb of joy is not amiss
To hymn his new-rejuvenescent fame:

> O thunder-thanks! One hundred fifty-four:
> Though grandly ample—wish you'd written more!

Final Thoughts:
On Proofing **Shakespair**

𝔄 pile of paper lies upon the desk
And cannot let me sit, but bids me move.
To miss an error? Possibly grotesque
Effects of inadvertency might prove.

The 'prentice poet care may well behoove.
For who's the perfect master of the craft?
Our thinking likes to travel in a groove...
But can't perfectionism drive you daft?

My manuscript I never can revisit
Without encountering corrections needed.
That isn't really too obsessive, is it?
The call of caution can't remain unheeded.

    I've got to check the rhythms and the rhymes
    Or William will object a million times.

Index of Personal Names in the Replies

Achilles, 75
Adam, 163
Adonai, 195
Adonis, 106, 107, 195
Ajax, 201
Alden, John, 269
Anne (St.), 41
Apollo, 67, 307
Aristotle, 93, 231
Arthur, King, 201
Augustine (St.), 303

Bacchus, 41
Beatrice, 43
Blake, William, 49, 69
Boaz, 195
Byron, George Gordon, Lord, 39, 197

Caesar, 201
Carlyle, Thomas, 99
Charon, 75
Coleridge, Samuel Taylor, 113, 207
Cowley, Abraham, 45
Crashaw, Richard, 45
Cupid, 303, 305, 307

da Vinci, *see* Leonardo

Dante, 43, 183, 203, 213, 219
David, 15, 111, 233
Dian(a), 213
Diotima, 83
Donne, John, 45

Echo, 7
Elizabeth, Queen, 215
Euripides, 163
Eve, 186, 187, 191

Fascinans, 303
Ficino, Marsilio, 95
Fließ, Wilhelm, 225
Fortuna, 223
Freud, Sigmund, 225, 287

Gemini, 29, 35
Goethe, Johann Wolfgang von, 149, 199
Gorgon, 47
Gregor (Samsa), 117

Hamlet, 229
Hannah, 19
Hawthorne, Nathaniel, 225
Hector, 201

Helen, 106, 107, 275
Heraclitus, 91
Herbert, George, 45
Hercules, 201
Hermes (Trismegistus), 67, 245
Hesiod, 137
Hesper-Phosphor, 265
Homer, 163
Horace, 111
Hyacinth, 209, 307

James, King, 215
Jesus, 213
John (St.), 41
Jonathan, 111, 233
Juliet, 55
Jupiter, 247

Kafka, Franz, 117
Keats, John, 53, 197, 207

Lacan, Jacques, 137
Launcelot, Sir, 201
Leoline, Sir, 113
Leonardo, 41
Lincoln, Abraham, 289
Longfellow, Henry Wadsworth, 269

Masoch, see Sacher-Masoch
Melville, Herman, 225
Memory (Mnemosyne), 197
Mercury, 97
Milton, John, 137, 149, 231, 239
Mona Lisa, 41
Moses, 213

Muhammad, 157
Mullins, Priscilla, 269

Narcissus, 7
Neptune, 161

Odin, 181
Ovid, 137, 197

Pater, Walter, 153
Penelope, 31
Pericles, 163
Petrarch, Francesco, 65
Philomel, 204, 205
Phoebus, 59, 67, 209, 307
Plato, 29, 77, 93, 95, 107, 211
Plotinus, 95
Pluto, 219
Plutus, 219
Prospero, 257
Proust, Marcel, 153
Pushkin, Alexander, 279
Pythagoras, 17, 143

René, King (of Provence), 201
Ricketts, Ed, 225
Roland, Lord, 113
Romeo, 55
Ruth, 195, 265

Sacher-Masoch, Leopold Ritter von, 117
Sappho, 77
Sarah, 19
Sartre, Jean-Paul, 89
Satan, 39
Saturn, 197, 247

Schopenhauer, Artur, 259, 271
Sheherazade, 277
Shelley, Percy Bysshe, 105, 137, 207
Sidney, Sir Philip, 65
Socrates, 83
Solomon, 23, 255
Spinoza, Baruch, 105, 185
Standish, Miles, 269
Steinbeck, John, 225
Stevens, Wallace, 209
Sybil(s), 41
Syrinx, 209

Tchaikovsky, Peter Ilyich, 297

Tennyson, Alfred, Lord, 37, 153
Thea, 197
Thomas, Dylan, 293
Traherne, Thomas, 45
Tyutchev, Fyodor, 171

Ulysses, 31, 113

Vaughan, Henry, 45
Venus, 265
Venus (in Furs), 117

Wordsworth, William, 221

Zuleika, 199

Made in United States
Orlando, FL
12 December 2024